Collected
Black Women's
Poetry

THE SCHOMBURG LIBRARY OF
NINETEENTH-CENTURY BLACK WOMEN WRITERS

General Editor, Henry Louis Gates, Jr.

Titles are listed chronologically; collections that include works published over a span of years are listed according to the publication date of their initial work.

Collected
Black Women's Poetry

Volume 4

Edited by
JOAN R. SHERMAN

ை ை ை

ை ை ை

New York   Oxford
OXFORD UNIVERSITY PRESS
1988

Oxford University Press

Oxford   New York   Toronto
Delhi   Bombay   Calcutta   Madras   Karachi
Petaling Jaya   Singapore   Hong Kong   Tokyo
Nairobi   Dar es Salaam   Cape Town
Melbourne   Auckland
and associated companies in
Beirut   Berlin   Ibadan   Nicosia

Copyright © 1988 by Oxford University Press, Inc.

Published by Oxford University Press, Inc.,
200 Madison Avenue, New York, New York 10016

Library of Congress Cataloging-in-Publication Data
Collected black women's poetry.
(The Schomburg library of nineteenth-century black
women writers)
1. American poetry—Afro-American authors.
2. American poetry—Women authors.   3. American poetry—
19th century.   4. Afro-American women—Poetry.
I. Sherman, Joan Rita.   I. Series.
PS591.N4C57   1988   811'.008'09287   87-20379
ISBN 0-19-505256-0 (v. 4)
ISBN 0-19-505267-6 (set)

The
Schomburg Library
of
Nineteenth-Century
Black Women Writers
is
Dedicated
in Memory
of
PAULINE AUGUSTA COLEMAN GATES

1916–1987

PUBLISHER'S NOTE

FOREWORD
In Her Own Write

Henry Louis Gates, Jr.

One muffled strain in the Silent South, a jarring chord and a vague and uncomprehended cadenza has been and still is the Negro. And of that muffled chord, the one mute and voiceless note has been the sadly expectant Black Woman, ...

The "other side" has not been represented by one who "lives there." And not many can more sensibly realize and more accurately tell the weight and the fret of the "long dull pain" than the open-eyed but hitherto voiceless Black Woman of America.

. . . as our Caucasian barristers are not to blame if they cannot *quite* put themselves in the dark man's place, neither should the dark man be wholly expected fully and adequately to reproduce the exact Voice of the Black Woman.

—ANNA JULIA COOPER, *A Voice From the South* (1892)

The birth of the Afro-American literary tradition occurred in 1773, when Phillis Wheatley published a book of poetry. Despite the fact that her book garnered for her a remarkable amount of attention, Wheatley's journey to the printer had been a most arduous one. Sometime in 1772, a young African girl walked demurely into a room in Boston to undergo an oral examination, the results of which would determine the direction of her life and work. Perhaps she was shocked upon entering the appointed room. For there, perhaps gathered in a semicircle, sat eighteen of Boston's most notable citizens. Among them were John Erving, a prominent Boston merchant; the Reverend Charles Chauncy, pastor of the Tenth Congregational Church; and John Hancock, who would later gain fame for his signature on the Declaration of Independence. At the center of this group was His Excellency, Thomas Hutchinson, governor of Massachusetts, with Andrew Oliver, his lieutenant governor, close by his side.

Why had this august group been assembled? Why had it seen fit to summon this young African girl, scarcely eighteen years old, before it? This group of "the most respectable Characters in *Boston*," as it would later define itself, had assembled to question closely the African adolescent on the slender sheaf of poems that she claimed to have "written by herself." We can only speculate on the nature of the questions posed to the fledgling poet. Perhaps they asked her to identify and explain—for all to hear—exactly who were the Greek and Latin gods and poets alluded to so frequently in her work. Perhaps they asked her to conjugate a verb in Latin or even to translate randomly selected passages from the Latin, which she and her master, John Wheatley, claimed that she "had made some Progress in." Or perhaps they asked her to recite from memory key passages from the texts of John Milton and Alexander Pope, the two poets by whom the African claimed to be most directly influenced. We do not know.

We do know, however, that the African poet's responses were more than sufficient to prompt the eighteen august gentlemen to compose, sign, and publish a two-paragraph "Attestation," an open letter "To the Publick" that prefaces Phillis Wheatley's book and that reads in part:

> We whose Names are under-written, do assure the World, that the Poems specified in the following Page, were (as we

verily believe) written by Phillis, a young Negro Girl, who was but a few Years since, brought an uncultivated Barbarian from *Africa,* and has ever since been, and now is, under the Disadvantage of serving as a Slave in a Family in this Town. She has been examined by some of the best Judges, and is thought qualified to write them.

So important was this document in securing a publisher for Wheatley's poems that it forms the signal element in the prefatory matter preceding her *Poems on Various Subjects, Religious and Moral,* published in London in 1773.

Without the published "Attestation," Wheatley's publisher claimed, few would believe that an African could possibly have written poetry all by herself. As the eighteen put the matter clearly in their letter, "Numbers would be ready to suspect they were not really the Writings of Phillis." Wheatley and her master, John Wheatley, had attempted to publish a similar volume in 1772 in Boston, but Boston publishers had been incredulous. One year later, "Attestation" in hand, Phillis Wheatley and her master's son, Nathaniel Wheatley, sailed for England, where they completed arrangements for the publication of a volume of her poems with the aid of the Countess of Huntington and the Earl of Dartmouth.

This curious anecdote, surely one of the oddest oral examinations on record, is only a tiny part of a larger, and even more curious, episode in the Enlightenment. Since the beginning of the sixteenth century, Europeans had wondered aloud whether or not the African "species of men," as they were most commonly called, *could* ever create formal literature, could ever master "the arts and sciences." If they could, the argument ran, then the African variety of humanity was fundamentally related to the European variety. If not, then it seemed clear that the African was destined by nature to be a slave. This was the burden shouldered by Phillis Wheatley when she successfully defended herself and the authorship of her book against counterclaims and doubts.

Indeed, with her successful defense, Wheatley launched two traditions at once—the black American literary tradition *and* the black woman's literary tradition. If it is extraordinary that not just one but both of these traditions were founded simultaneously by a black woman—certainly an event unique in the history of literature—it is also ironic that this important fact of common, coterminous literary origins seems to have escaped most scholars.

That the progenitor of the black literary tradition was a woman means, in the most strictly literal sense, that all subsequent black writers have evolved in a matrilinear line of descent, and that each, consciously or unconsciously, has extended and revised a canon whose foundation was the poetry of a black woman. Early black writers seem to have been keenly aware of Wheatley's founding role, even if most of her white reviewers were more concerned with the implications of her race than her gender. Jupiter Hammon, for example, whose 1760 broadside "An Evening Thought. Salvation by Christ, With Penitential Cries" was the first individual poem published by a black American, acknowledged Wheatley's influence by selecting her as the subject of his second broadside, "An Address to Miss Phillis Wheatly [*sic*], Ethiopian Poetess, in Boston," which was published at Hartford in 1778. And George Moses Horton, the second Afro-American to publish a book of poetry in English (1829), brought out in 1838 an edition of his *Poems By A Slave* bound together with Wheatley's work. Indeed, for fifty-six years, between 1773 and 1829, when Horton published *The Hope of Liberty*, Wheatley was the *only* black person to have published a book of imaginative literature in English. So

central was this black woman's role in the shaping of the
Afro-American literary tradition that, as one historian has
maintained, the history of the reception of Phillis Wheatley's
poetry *is* the history of Afro-American literary criticism. Well
into the nineteenth century, Wheatley and the black literary
tradition were the same entity.

But Wheatley is not the only black woman writer who
stands as a pioneering figure in Afro-American literature.
Just as Wheatley gave birth to the genre of black poetry, Ann
Plato was the first Afro-American to publish a book of essays
(1841) and Harriet E. Wilson was the first black person to
publish a novel in the United States (1859).

Despite this pioneering role of black women in the tradi-
tion, however, many of their contributions before this cen-
tury have been all but lost or unrecognized. As Hortense
Spillers observed as recently as 1983,

> With the exception of a handful of autobiographical narratives
> from the nineteenth century, the black woman's realities are
> virtually suppressed until the period of the Harlem Renais-
> sance and later. Essentially the black woman as artist, as
> intellectual spokesperson for her own cultural apprenticeship,
> has not existed before, for anyone. At the source of [their]
> own symbol-making task, [the community of black women
> writers] confronts, therefore, a tradition of work that is quite
> recent, its continuities, broken and sporadic.

Until now, it has been extraordinarily difficult to establish
the formal connections between early black women's writing
and that of the present, precisely because our knowledge of
their work has been broken and sporadic. Phillis Wheatley,
for example, while certainly the most reprinted and discussed
poet in the tradition, is also one of the least understood. Ann
Plato's seminal work, *Essays* (which includes biographies and
poems), has not been reprinted since it was published a cen-

tury and a half ago. And Harriet Wilson's *Our Nig,* her
compelling novel of a black woman's expanding conscious-
ness in a racist Northern antebellum environment, never re-
ceived even *one* review or comment at a time when virtually
all works written by black people were heralded by abolition-
ists as salient arguments against the existence of human slav-
ery. Many of the books reprinted in this set experienced a
similar fate, the most dreadful fate for an author: that of
being ignored then relegated to the obscurity of the rare book
section of a university library. We can only wonder how
many other texts in the black woman's tradition have been
lost to this generation of readers or remain unclassified or
uncatalogued and, hence, unread.

This was not always so, however. Black women writers
dominated the final decade of the nineteenth century, perhaps
spurred to publish by an 1886 essay entitled "The Coming
American Novelist," which was published in *Lippincott's
Monthly Magazine* and written by "A Lady From Philadel-
phia." This pseudonymous essay argued that the "Great
American Novel" would be written by a black person. Her
argument is so curious that it deserves to be repeated:

> When we come to formulate our demands of the Coming
> American Novelist, we will agree that he must be native-
> born. His ancestors may come from where they will, but we
> must give him a birthplace and have the raising of him. Still,
> the longer his family has been here the better he will represent
> us. Suppose he should have no country but ours, no traditions
> but those he has learned here, no longings apart from us, no
> future except in our future—the orphan of the world, he
> finds with us his home. And with all this, suppose he refuses
> to be fused into that grand conglomerate we call the "Amer-
> ican type." With us, he is not of us. He is original, he has
> humor, he is tender, he is passive and fiery, he has been

taught what we call justice, and he has his own opinion about
it. He has suffered everything a poet, a dramatist, a novelist
need suffer before he comes to have his lips anointed. And
with it all he is in one sense a spectator, a little out of the
race. How would these conditions go towards forming an
original development? In a word, suppose the coming novelist
is of African origin? When one comes to consider the subject,
there is no improbability in it. One thing is certain,—our
great novel will not be written by the typical American.

An atypical American, indeed. Not only would the great
American novel be written by an African-American, it would
be written by an African-American *woman:*

> Yet farther: I have used the generic masculine pronoun
> because it is convenient; but Fate keeps revenge in store. It
> was a woman who, taking the wrongs of the African as her
> theme, wrote the novel that awakened the world to their
> reality, and why should not the coming novelist be a woman
> as well as an African? She—the woman of that race—has
> some claims on Fate which are not yet paid up.

It is these claims on fate that we seek to pay by publishing
The Schomburg Library of Nineteenth-Century Black Women
Writers.

This theme would be repeated by several black women
authors, most notably by Anna Julia Cooper, a prototypical
black feminist whose 1892 *A Voice From the South* can be
considered to be one of the original texts of the black fem-
inist movement. It was Cooper who first analyzed the fal-
lacy of referring to "the Black man" when speaking of black
people and who argued that just as white men cannot speak
through the consciousness of black men, neither can black
men "fully and adequately . . . reproduce the exact Voice of
the Black Woman." Gender and race, she argues, cannot be

conflated, except in the instance of a black woman's voice, and it is this voice which must be uttered and to which we must listen. As Cooper puts the matter so compellingly:

> It is not the intelligent woman vs. the ignorant woman; nor the white woman vs. the black, the brown, and the red,—it is not even the cause of woman vs. man. Nay, 'tis woman's strongest vindication for speaking that *the world needs to hear her voice*. It would be subversive of every human interest that the cry of one-half the human family be stifled. Woman in stepping from the pedestal of statue-like inactivity in the domestic shrine, and daring to think and move and speak,— to undertake to help shape, mold, and direct the thought of her age, is merely completing the circle of the world's vision. Hers is every interest that has lacked an interpreter and a defender. Her cause is linked with that of every agony that has been dumb—every wrong that needs a voice.
>
> It is no fault of man's that he has not been able to see truth from her standpoint. It does credit both to his head and heart that no greater mistakes have been committed or even wrongs perpetrated while she sat making tatting and snipping paper flowers. Man's own innate chivalry and the mutual interde-pendence of their interests have insured his treating her cause, in the main at least, as his own. And he is pardonably surprised and even a little chagrined, perhaps, to find his legislation not considered "perfectly lovely" in every respect. But in any case his work is only impoverished by her remaining dumb. The world has had to limp along with the wobbling gait and one-sided hesitancy of a man with one eye. Suddenly the bandage is removed from the other eye and the whole body is filled with light. It sees a circle where before it saw a segment. The darkened eye restored, every member rejoices with it.

The myopic sight of the darkened eye can only be restored when the full range of the black woman's voice, with its own special timbres and shadings, remains mute no longer.

Similarly, Victoria Earle Matthews, an author of short stories and essays, and a cofounder in 1896 of the National Association of Colored Women, wrote in her stunning essay, "The Value of Race Literature" (1895), that "when the literature of our race is developed, it will of necessity be different in all essential points of greatness, true heroism and real Christianity from what we may at the present time, for convenience, call American literature." Matthews argued that this great tradition of Afro-American literature would be the textual outlet "for the unnaturally suppressed inner lives which our people have been compelled to lead." Once these "unnaturally suppressed inner lives" of black people are unveiled, no "grander diffusion of mental light" will shine more brightly, she concludes, than that of the articulate Afro-American woman:

> And now comes the question, What part shall we women play in the Race Literature of the future? . . . within the compass of one small journal ["Woman's Era"] we have struck out a new line of departure—a journal, a record of Race interests gathered from all parts of the United States, carefully selected, moistened, winnowed and garnered by the ablest intellects of educated colored women, shrinking at no lofty theme, shirking no serious duty, aiming at every possible excellence, and determined to do their part in the future uplifting of the race.
>
> If twenty women, by their concentrated efforts in one literary movement, can meet with such success as has engendered, planned out, and so successfully consummated this convention, what much more glorious results, what wider spread success, what grander diffusion of mental light will not come forth at the bidding of the enlarged hosts of women writers, already called into being by the stimulus of your efforts?
>
> And here let me speak one word for my journalistic sisters

who have already entered the broad arena of journalism. Before the "Woman's Era" had come into existence, no one except themselves can appreciate the bitter experience and sore disappointments under which they have at all times been compelled to pursue their chosen vocations.

If their brothers of the press have had their difficulties to contend with, I am here as a sister journalist to state, from the fullness of knowledge, that their task has been an easy one compared with that of the colored woman in journalism.

Woman's part in Race Literature, as in Race building, is the most important part and has been so in all ages. . . . All through the most remote epochs she has done her share in literature. . . .

One of the most important aspects of this set is the republication of the salient texts from 1890 to 1910, which literary historians could well call "The Black Woman's Era." In addition to Mary Helen Washington's definitive edition of Cooper's *A Voice From the South,* we have reprinted two novels by Amelia Johnson, Frances Harper's *Iola Leroy,* two novels by Emma Dunham Kelley, Alice Dunbar-Nelson's two impressive collections of short stories, and Pauline Hopkins's three serialized novels as well as her monumental novel, *Contending Forces*—all published between 1890 and 1910. Indeed, black women published more works of fiction in these two decades than black men had published in the previous half century. Nevertheless, this great achievement has been ignored.

Moreover, the writings of nineteenth-century Afro-American women in general have remained buried in obscurity, accessible only in research libraries or in overpriced and poorly edited reprints. Many of these books have never been reprinted at all; in some instances only one or two copies are extant. In these works of fiction, poetry, autobiography, biography, essays, and journalism resides the mind of the nineteenth-century Afro-American woman. Until these works are made readily available to teachers and their students, a significant segment of the black tradition will remain silent.

Oxford University Press, in collaboration with the Schomburg Center for Research in Black Culture, is publishing thirty volumes of these compelling works, each of which contains an introduction by an expert in the field. The set includes such rare texts as Johnson's *The Hazeley Family* and *Clarence and Corinne*, Plato's *Essays*, the most complete edition of Phillis Wheatley's poems and letters, Emma Dunham Kelley's pioneering novel *Megda*, several previously unpublished stories and a novel by Alice Dunbar-Nelson, and the first collected volumes of Pauline Hopkins's three serialized novels and Frances Harper's poetry. We also present four volumes of poetry by such women as Mary Eliza Tucker Lambert, Adah Menken, Josephine Heard, and Maggie Johnson. Numerous slave and spiritual narratives, a newly discovered novel—*Four Girls at Cottage City*—by Emma Dunham Kelley (-Hawkins), and the first American edition of *Wonderful Adventures of Mrs. Seacole in Many Lands* are also among the texts included.

In addition to resurrecting the works of black women authors, it is our hope that this set will facilitate the resurrection of the Afro-American woman's literary tradition itself by unearthing its nineteenth-century roots. In the works of Nella Larsen and Jessie Fauset, Zora Neale Hurston and Ann Petry, Lorraine Hansberry and Gwendolyn Brooks, Paule Marshall and Toni Cade Bambara, Audre Lorde and Rita Dove, Toni Morrison and Alice Walker, Gloria Naylor and Jamaica Kincaid, these roots have branched luxuriantly. The eighteenth- and nineteenth-century authors whose works are presented in this set founded and nurtured the black women's literary tradition, which must be revived, explicated, analyzed, and debated before we can understand more completely the formal shaping of this tradition within a tradition, a coded literary universe through which, regrettably, we are only just beginning to navigate our way. As Anna Cooper said nearly one hundred years ago, we have been blinded by the loss of sight in one eye and have therefore been unable to detect the full *shape* of the Afro-American literary tradition.

Literary works configure into a tradition not because of some mystical collective unconscious determined by the biology of race or gender, but because writers read other writers and *ground* their representations of experience in models of language provided largely by other writers to whom they feel akin. It is through this mode of literary revision, amply evident in the *texts* themselves—in formal echoes, recast metaphors, even in parody—that a "tradition" emerges and defines itself.

This is formal bonding, and it is only through formal bonding that we can know a literary tradition. The collective publication of these works by black women now, for the first time, makes it possible for scholars and critics, male and female, black and white, to *demonstrate* that black women writers read, and revised, other black women writers. To demonstrate this set of formal literary relations is to demonstrate that sexuality, race, and gender are both the condition and the basis of *tradition*—but tradition as found in discrete acts of language use.

A word is in order about the history of this set. For the past decade, I have taught a course, first at Yale and then at Cornell, entitled "Black Women and Their Fictions," a course that I inherited from Toni Morrison, who developed it in the mid-1970s for Yale's Program in Afro-American Studies. Although the course was inspired by the remarkable accomplishments of black women novelists since 1970, I gradually extended its beginning date to the late nineteenth century, studying Frances Harper's *Iola Leroy* and Anna Julia Cooper's *A Voice From the South,* both published in 1892. With the discovery of Harriet E. Wilson's seminal novel, *Our Nig* (1859), and Jean Yellin's authentication of Harriet Jacobs's brilliant slave narrative, *Incidents in the Life of a Slave Girl* (1861), a survey course spanning over a century and a quarter emerged.

But the discovery of *Our Nig,* as well as the interest in nineteenth-century black women's writing that this discovery generated, convinced me that even the most curious and diligent scholars knew very little of the extensive history of the creative writings of Afro-American women before 1900. Indeed, most scholars of Afro-American literature had never even read most of the books published by black women, simply because these books—of poetry, novels, short stories, essays, and autobiography—were mostly accessible only in rare book sections of university libraries. For reasons unclear to me even today, few of these marvelous renderings of the Afro-American woman's consciousness were reprinted in the late 1960s and early 1970s, when so many other texts of the Afro-American literary tradition were resurrected from the dark and silent graveyard of the out-of-print and were reissued in facsimile editions aimed at the hungry readership for canonical texts in the nascent field of black studies.

So, with the help of several superb research assistants—including David Curtis, Nicola Shilliam, Wendy Jones, Sam Otter, Janadas Devan, Suvir Kaul, Cynthia Bond, Elizabeth Alexander, and Adele Alexander—and with the expert advice of scholars such as William Robinson, William Andrews, Mary Helen Washington, Maryemma Graham, Jean Yellin, Houston A. Baker, Jr., Richard Yarborough, Hazel Carby, Joan R. Sherman, Frances Foster, and William French, dozens of bibliographies were used to compile a list of books written or narrated by black women mostly before 1910. Without the assistance provided through this shared experience of scholarship, the scholar's true legacy, this project could not have been conceived. As the list grew, I was struck by how very many of these titles that I, for example, had never even heard of, let alone read, such as Ann Plato's *Essays*, Louisa Picquet's slave narrative, or Amelia Johnson's two novels, *Clarence and Corinne* and *The Hazeley Family*. Through our research with the Black Periodical Fiction and Poetry Project (funded by NEH and the Ford Foundation), I also realized that several novels by black women, including three works of fiction by Pauline Hopkins, had been serialized in black periodicals, but had never been collected and published as books. Nor had the several books of poetry published by black women, such as the prolific Frances E. W. Harper, been collected and edited. When I discovered still another "lost" novel by an Afro-American woman (*Four Girls at Cottage City*, published in 1898 by Emma Dunham Kelley-Hawkins), I decided to attempt to edit a collection of reprints of these works and to publish them as a "library" of black women's writings, in part so that I could read them myself.

Convincing university and trade publishers to undertake this project proved to be a difficult task. Despite the commercial success of *Our Nig* and of the several reprint series of women's works (such as Virago, the Beacon Black Women Writers Series, and Rutgers' American Women Writers Series), several presses rejected the project as "too large," "too limited," or as "commercially unviable." Only two publishers recognized the viability and the import of the project and, of these, Oxford's commitment to publish the titles simultaneously as a set made the press's offer irresistible.

While attempting to locate original copies of these exceedingly rare books, I discovered that most of the texts were housed at the Schomburg Center for Research in Black Culture, a branch of The New York Public Library, under the direction of Howard Dodson. Dodson's infectious enthusiasm for the project and his generous collaboration, as well as that of his stellar staff (especially Diana Lachatanere, Sharon Howard, Ellis Haizip, Richard Newman, and Betty Gubert), led to a joint publishing initiative that produced this set as part of the Schomburg's major fund-raising campaign. Without Dodson's foresight and generosity of spirit, the set would not have materialized. Without William P. Sisler's masterful editorship at Oxford and his staff's careful attention to detail, the set would have remained just another grand idea that tends to languish in a scholar's file cabinet.

I would also like to thank Dr. Michael Winston and Dr. Thomas C. Battle, Vice-President of Academic Affairs and the Director of the Moorland-Spingarn Research Center (respectively) at Howard University, for their unending encouragement, support, and collaboration in this project, and Esme E. Bhan at Howard for her meticulous research and bibliographical skills. In addition, I would like to acknowledge the aid of the staff at the libraries of Duke University, Cornell University (especially Tom Weissinger and Donald Eddy), the Boston Public Library, the Western Reserve Historical Society, the Library of Congress, and Yale University. Linda Robbins, Marion Osmun, Sarah Flanagan, and Gerard Case, all members of the staff at Oxford, were

extraordinarily effective at coordinating, editing, and pro-
ducing the various segments of each text in the set. Candy
Ruck, Nina de Tar, and Phillis Molock expertly typed reams
of correspondence and manuscripts connected to the project.

I would also like to express my gratitude to my colleagues
who edited and introduced the individual titles in the set.
Without their attention to detail, their willingness to meet
strict deadlines, and their sheer enthusiasm for this project,
the set could not have been published. But finally and ulti-
mately, I would hope that the publication of the set would
help to generate even more scholarly interest in the black
women authors whose work is presented here. Struggling
against the seemingly insurmountable barriers of racism *and*
sexism, while often raising families and fulfilling full-time
professional obligations, these women managed nevertheless
to record their thoughts and feelings and to *testify* to all who
dare read them that the will to harness the power of collective
endurance and survival is the will to write.

The Schomburg Library of Nineteenth-Century Black
Women Writers is dedicated in memory of Pauline Augusta
Coleman Gates, who died in the spring of 1987. It was she
who inspired in me the love of learning and the love of lit-
erature. I have encountered in the books of this set no will
more determined, no courage more noble, no mind more
sublime, no self more celebratory of the achievements of all
Afro-American women, and indeed of life itself, than her
own.

A NOTE FROM
THE SCHOMBURG CENTER

Howard Dodson

The Schomburg Center for Research in Black Culture, The
New York Public Library, is pleased to join with Dr. Henry
Louis Gates and Oxford University Press in presenting The
Schomburg Library of Nineteenth-Century Black Women
Writers. This thirty-volume set includes the work of a gen-
eration of black women whose writing has only been available
previously in rare book collections. The materials reprinted
in twenty-four of the thirty volumes are drawn from the
unique holdings of the Schomburg Center.

A research unit of The New York Public Library, the
Schomburg Center has been in the forefront of those insti-
tutions dedicated to collecting, preserving, and providing
access to the records of the black past. In the course of its
two generations of acquisition and conservation activity, the
Center has amassed collections totaling more than 5 million
items. They include over 100,000 bound volumes, 85,000
reels and sets of microforms, 300 manuscript collections
containing some 3.5 million items, 300,000 photographs and
extensive holdings of prints, sound recordings, film and
videotape, newspapers, artworks, artifacts, and other book
and nonbook materials. Together they vividly document the
history and cultural heritages of people of African descent
worldwide.

Though established some sixty-two years ago, the Center's
book collections date from the sixteenth century. Its oldest
item, an Ethiopian Coptic Tunic, dates from the eighth or
ninth century. Rare materials, however, are most available

for the nineteenth-century African-American experience. It is
from these holdings that the majority of the titles selected for
inclusion in this set are drawn.

The nineteenth century was a formative period in African-
American literary and cultural history. Prior to the Civil
War, the majority of black Americans living in the United
States were held in bondage. Law and practice forbade teach-
ing them to read or write. Even after the war, many of the
impediments to learning and literary productivity remained.
Nevertheless, black men and women of the nineteenth century
persevered in both areas. Moreover, more African-Americans
than we yet realize turned their observations, feelings, social
viewpoints, and creative impulses into published works. In
time, this nineteenth-century printed record included poetry,
short stories, histories, novels, autobiographies, social criti-
cism, and theology, as well as economic and philosophical
treatises. Unfortunately, much of this body of literature
remained, until very recently, relatively inaccessible to twentieth-
century scholars, teachers, creative artists, and others inter-
ested in black life. Prior to the late 1960s, most Americans
(black as well as white) had never heard of these nineteenth-
century authors, much less read their works.

The civil rights and black power movements created un-
precedented interest in the thought, behavior, and achieve-
ments of black people. Publishers responded by revising
traditional texts, introducing the American public to a new
generation of African-American writers, publishing a variety
of thematic anthologies, and reprinting a plethora of "classic
texts" in African-American history, literature, and art. The
reprints usually appeared as individual titles or in a series of
bound volumes or microform formats.

The Schomburg Center, which has a long history of supporting publishing that deals with the history and culture of Africans in diaspora, became an active participant in many of the reprint revivals of the 1960s. Since hard copies of original printed works are the preferred formats for producing facsimile reproductions, publishers frequently turned to the Schomburg Center for copies of these original titles. In addition to providing such material, Schomburg Center staff members offered advice and consultation, wrote introductions, and occasionally entered into formal copublishing arrangements in some projects.

Most of the nineteenth-century titles reprinted during the 1960s, however, were by and about black men. A few black women were included in the longer series, but works by lesser known black women were generally overlooked. The Schomburg Library of Nineteenth-Century Black Women Writers is both a corrective to these previous omissions and an important contribution to Afro-American literary history in its own right. Through this collection of volumes, the thoughts, perspectives, and creative abilities of nineteenth-century African-American women, as captured in books and pamphlets published in large part before 1910, are again being made available to the general public. The Schomburg Center is pleased to be a part of this historic endeavor.

I would like to thank Professor Gates for initiating this project. Thanks are due both to him and Mr. William P. Sisler of Oxford University Press for giving the Schomburg Center an opportunity to play such a prominent role in the set. Thanks are also due to my colleagues at The New York Public Library and the Schomburg Center, especially Dr. Vartan Gregorian, Richard De Gennaro, Paul Fasana, Betsy

Pinover, Richard Newman, Diana Lachatanere, Glenderlyn Johnson, and Harold Anderson for their assistance and support. I can think of no better way of demonstrating than in this set the role the Schomburg Center plays in assuring that the black heritage will be available for future generations.

CONTENTS

INTRODUCTION

The four poets in this volume represent the range of poetic attitudes characteristic of turn-of-the-century black writers: religious (Heard); romantic (Bibb); nostalgic (Johnson); and upward bound (Linden).

The last selection in *Morning Glories* (1890), in a group of ten "Obituaries," is "An Epitaph" that Josephine Delphine (Henderson) Heard (1861–19?) seems to have prepared for herself: her tombstone would read, "She hath done what she could." Regrettably, in regard to poetry, what she could do was uniformly weak. Heard's seventy-eight verses lack originality of topic and execution; emotions never rise above sentimentality and religious piety; language is insipid and sometimes unintelligible.

An educated woman and teacher, Heard was aware of the world around her. In "Tennyson's Poems" she compares herself to the English bard, and a tribute, "To Whittier," requests this poet's autograph; Whittier's response appears in Heard's "Appendix" of congratulatory letters. Other verses compliment Frederick Douglass, her "Moses of the negro race," Fanny Jackson Coppin, General Robert Small, and several black clergymen, including Bishop Payne of Wilberforce and her husband, AME Bishop William Henry Heard; these verses, with two stock poems on "The Race Problem," are Heard's only recognition of her race. Occasionally she mulls over abstractions as in "Hope," "a vain, delusive maiden," "Fame," "Truth," and "The Birth of Time." But the great majority of Heard's "morning glories" talk of love, lost and found, and God, here and in eternity. The poems' titles tell the whole story: "The Parting Kiss," "Slumbering Passion," "He Comes not To-Night," and "I Love Thee!" are some of the love notes; "Sunshine after Cloud," "Eternity," "Hope Thou in God," and "The Birth of Jesus" are some of the devotional pieces. It is difficult among these repetitive verses to find a fresh idea or imaginative phrase. "She hath done what she could."

Eloise Alberta Veronica Bibb (1878–1927) was born in New Orleans to Charles H. and Catherine Adele Bibb. She spent her childhood and received her early schooling in New Orleans, where her father was a customs inspector. After attending the Oberlin Academy preparatory department from 1899 until 1901, she taught in the public schools of New Orleans for two years. She matriculated at Howard University in 1903 and graduated from its Teachers' College in January 1908. In April of that year, Bibb became head resident of the Colored Social Settlement in Washington, D.C., a post she held until 1911.

In Chicago, on August 14, 1911, Bibb married Noah D. Thompson, a widower. They moved to Los Angeles where both worked actively for the Catholic church, and Mrs. Thompson was a special feature writer for the Los Angeles *Sunday Times* and the *Morning Sun*. She contributed articles and poetry to popular magazines, among them *Out West* and *Tidings*, the official organ of the diocese of Monterey and Los Angeles. The Thompsons had one child, Noah Murphy, and they lived in Los Angeles throughout the 1920s.

Eloise Bibb was a precocious writer; her *Poems* (1895) appeared when she was seventeen. Thus it is not surprising that half the verses in this slim volume are romantic narratives of star-crossed lovers and agonized heroes. These generally commence with descriptions of time and weather conditions such as "The morn has risen clear and bright" or " 'Twas eve in sunny Italy." They proceed to a story line that may be either complicated and illogical, as in "Imogene," or, more often, single and smoothly developed with sustained suspense, as in "Destiny," "The Hermit," and "Gerarda." Gerarda, for example, is a typical young maiden who loves Neville, the organist who played at her wedding. For years she suffers and laments their separation until one day Neville reappears and kisses Gerarda: "And at the touch the fire of love,/So pure as to come from above,/Consumes his heart and racks his brain,/With longing fear and infinite pain." The lady, equally moved, sends him away, for she is "alas! a wedded wife." But a fortunate fire soon destroys her home, husband, and family; Neville rescues Gerarda from the flames, and they live happily ever after.

Other lovers, including those in "Captain Smith and Pocahontas," are similarly rewarded, but disasters of Gothic-novel dimensions plague the lovers of "The Vestal Virgin" and "A Tale of Italy." Although her lovers' catastrophes differ, Bibb's characters vary in little more than their names from tale to tale, and inevitably the poetic sentiments are those of a young girl in love with love, the more tempestuous the better.

In other verses on biblical and historical subjects such as "The Wandering Jew," "Eliza, in 'Uncle Tom's Cabin,' " "Anne Boleyn," and "Judith," Bibb is content with a pleasing simplicity of statement; these narratives are metrically even, consistent in tone and story line, and free from excessive sentimental embroidery. Additional short lyrics, including accolades to nature and to luminaries like Frederick Douglass and Al-

ice Ruth Moore (Dunbar), remain trite and weak. It is in
the longer narratives that Bibb demonstrates a breadth of in-
terest and talent for versifying that is unusual in so young a
poet.

The two-part title of Virginia-born Maggie Pogue Johnson's
volume (1910) reveals its contents and her intentions. Emu-
lating Dunbar, the "Poet of Our Race" whose memory she
reveres, Johnson speaks in two voices: her *Virginia Dreams*
are dialect poems, brimming with local color, folklore, and
nostalgia, while *Lyrics for the Idle Hour* treat a variety of
topics in standard English.

Johnson's debt to Dunbar, and perhaps to another Virginia
poet, Daniel Webster Davis, seems strong in her portraits of
"lowly life." An evocation of lazy summer days recalls Dun-
bar's "Song of Summer," and Johnson's celebrations of
"Krismas Dinnah," killing the turkey for Thanksgiving, a
leap-year party, and the mouthwatering bounty of down-home
foods—chicken, dumplings, baked beans, greens, bacon,
watermelon, pork chops—echo popular dialect poems like
Dunbar's "The Party." Johnson often records the black ver-
nacular accurately, maintains musical iambics with ease, and
marshalls lively details to build humor and picturesqueness,
as in her gently satirical run-down of superstitions or in the
affectionate recollection of songs and speeches at church. Fre-
quently, women speak in these verses: They comment on
fashion or "men folks"; they appear as mothers calling and
scolding kids at mealtime, or as an old maid, looked down
on by all, who asserts her pride.

Johnson seems aware that most of her dialect verses are
indeed "Virginia dreams" of a long-ago and far-away har-
monious world, for she also brings the black folk out of the

past into Booker T. Washington's orbit: Sister Johnson preaches the upward-bound philosophy in church, and a young man, in "To See Ol' Booker T.," sets off for Tuskegee to learn to read and plant cotton. Further, a few standard English poems encourage the Negro to be proud of his advances, helped by whites, to make good by going to college or taking up a trade, and to be ambitious and behave morally. In other "lyrics" of this volume, trivial topics—a lost Teddy Bear— and banal language dominate. In sum, Johnson's often charming sketches of life in old Virginia are her most successful verses.

The most interesting part of Mrs. Henry Linden's *Autobiography and Poems* (n.d.) is her "Autobiography," an inspirational saga of heroic striving, of poverty and bad luck overcome by her ingenuity, self-confidence, and hard work. By her own example, Mrs. Linden supports her advice to "dear readers": "With push, pluck and ambition and Christ as your leader, you will make life a success." To these necessary attributes she adds self-respect, "faith in your own ability," and the courage to fight for the right unto death.

In her poems, Linden lionizes Booker T. Washington, his "pluck and ambition," and devotes two dozen pieces to his gospel of self-improvement: she counsels the race to pay its debts, save money, buy homes, trust in and praise God, obey the law, improve the world, and follow all the precepts of her "Autobiography." In addition to Washington, Linden admires Teddy Roosevelt in the "song," "All We Ask is Justice"; she also praises Bishop Payne of Wilberforce, the departed Paul Laurence Dunbar, and the King and Queen of England.

Linden tells us she became active in club work in 1901,

eventually belonging to six clubs and becoming president of
two. More than a dozen of her verses praise and encourage
"noble colored women" and their club work. While she
identifies only a few clubs in verse, like the Household of
Ruth, the Phyllis [*sic*] Wheatley, and the Ohio State chapter
of the National Federation, she makes clear the crucial role
that all black women's clubs play in charitable and self-help
activities for the race.

Identical formulas for moving onward and upward inform
all of Linden's verse. Indeed, these pieces simply extend the
"Autobiography," for they are *prose* arranged in lines and
stanzas. The prose is end-rhymed, as in "The Y.M.C.A.":
"One of our race's greatest needs in this country today/Is a
number of well supported and managed Y.M.C.A."; gen-
erally, Linden's lines run on, as in "October is Here": "This
is our club work, to give to the needy as well as improve/
Our own minds, and to look after the sick and give homes/
To the children, and tell the poor mother to tell hers what to
do." The didacticisms closely resemble one another, giving a
reader no relief from tedium except puzzlement when mean-
ing is garbled:

> Now our lives vary like the seasons in reason,
> We are not all alike, and how could we be?
> Some like the fall, always gloomy and chilly,
> But once in awhile the sun shines in their home.
> ("The Fall is Here")

Linden's work has historical value for her insistence on the
power of black women—"the hand that rocks the cradle rules
the world," she quotes—as well as for her stress on the black
women's club movement and her wholehearted adoption of

Washington's self-help ethic. Otherwise, although she claims in "Cultivation" that "some of the best critics in the land/ Have indorsed me as a poet," modern readers will find her a remarkably strong, able woman and propagandist dedicated to the race's improvement, but no poet.

Collected
Black Women's
Poetry

Dedication.

To my devoted Husband, is this little
Book lovingly Dedicated:

GOD SPEED! Say I, and all Good Cheer,
    May fair winds fill thy sails—
Go proudly on thy Mission sent,
    Fearless of adverse gales.

                        J. D. H. H.

SPEAKER, PRINT,
LANCASTER, PA.

MORNING ✣ GLORIES

Truly Yours,
Josie D. Henderson Heard.

MORNING ✦ GLORIES

—✴ BY ✴—

JOSEPHINE D. (HENDERSON) HEARD,

Philadelphia, Penna.

MARCH 17, 1890

PREFACE.

Dear Friends:

Will you accept a Bunch of " MORNING GLORIES,"
freshly plucked and with the Dew Drops still upon them?
Coming, as they do, from a heart that desires to encourage
and inspire the youth of the Race to pure and noble
motives, to cheer the aged, may they find a welcome
beside the Brothers and Sisters, in prose and poetry,
which already adorn your homes.

THE AUTHOR.

PHILADELPHIA, Feb.   1890.

CONTENTS

CONTENTS.

PAGE.

PART III—THE RACE PROBLEM.

PART IV—OBITUARIES.

APPENDIX.

HISTORICAL SKETCH

—OF THE—

LIFE OF THE AUTHOR.

Mrs. Josie D. (Henderson) Heard was born in Salisbury, North Carolina, October 11th, 1861. Her parents, Lafayette and Annie M. Henderson, though slaves, were nominally free, being permitted to hire their time and live in another City, Charlotte, North Carolina.

At an early age, Josephine displayed her literary taste, and aptness to perform upon almost any musical instrument. As early as five years of age she could read, and was a source of general comfort to the aged neighbors, delighting to read the Scriptures to them.

She received her education in the schools at Charlotte, and having passed through them with credit, was sent to the Scotia Seminary at Concord, North Carolina, spending several years there. Her desire was to reach even a higher plain, and she was next sent to Bethany Institute, New York, passing with honors from its walls. She commenced teaching in the State which gave her birth; then in the State of South Carolina, at Maysville, Orangeburg and finally in Tennessee, at Covington, near Memphis.

In October, 1881, she became acquainted with the Rev. W. H. Heard, (now Presiding Elder of the Lancaster District, Philadelphia Conference,) who was then in the

U. S. R. Mail Service; and they were happily united in the Bonds of Matrimony in the year 1882.

Mrs. Heard evinced a fondness for poetry, and during her school days contributed to several leading evangelical periodicals. After her marriage she was encouraged by the Rt. Rev. Benj. Tucker Tanner, Rt. Rev. B. W. Arnett, and many other friends to give more time to it. At their solicitations she has ventured to bring to light these verses. She has some musical talent, having composed and written a piece of music which was played at the New Orleans Exposition, and which elicited much comment from the Democratic Press of the South.

W. H. H.

INTRODUCTION.

Bishop Benj. Tucker Tanner, D.D.

That he somewhat influenced the publication of "Morning Glories," gives the writer real pleasure; which is enhanced by the thought that he gladly accepted the invitation to write the Introduction.

For quite a quarter of a century, he has had much to do with the literary life of the people with whom h especially identified; as that life manifested itself in the production of papers, of monthly or quarterly magazines, of pamphlets and of books. He rejoices in the great progress made, both in quantity and quality. When he may be said to have begun his public literary career in 1868, there was scarcely more than two or three papers published by colored men. There are now quite as many hundred. Of magazines, there was none, now there are four. Of pamplets, upon very rare occasions, one was now and then issued. Now they appear, as do the leaves of autumn. And the same is true of books. A quarter of a century ago, a colored author was indeed a *rara avis*. Not so now, however, such individuals are fairly numerous.

What is true of the colored literature of the country, as to quantity, is equally true as to quality. On this score the most rapid advancement has also been made. *Incipient seholarship everywhere appearing upon the pages offered the public.*

On the line of Poety, we as a people, give sufficient evidence to show that the Muse is indeed no respecter of persons. That he is equally an admirer of *shade;* and although at times compelled in his approaches to us, to walk in unbeaten paths, yet he condescendingly comes, and inspires a music as sweet as is the wild honey of unkept hives. If any doubt, let him read, " MORNING GLORIES," to which these lines are to serve as an introduction. In rigid versification, the lines herein given, may here and there come short, but for brightness of imagination, for readiness of expression, and now and then for delicateness of touch, they are genuinely poetical ; clearly evincing a talent of no mean order.

We would wish that " MORNING GLORIES" might be received in the houses of our millions; showing thereby the party of the second part among us, stands ready to support the party of the first part, in all that tends to redeem the good name of the Race.

PART II.—MUSINGS

RETROSPECT.

I SAT alone at my window,
  While the pattering raindrops brought
Along with their music upon the roof,
  A lengthy train of thought.

I stepped aboard of it quickly,
  And rapidly on I sped,
Away to the scenes of my childhood days.
  I followed where fancy led.

I roamed the fragrant meadow,
  And through the silent wood ;
At last I came to the babbling brook,
  And sadly there I stood.

Into its clear water gazing
  I felt a strange, sweet spell
Enthral my being slowly
  As o'er my life it fell.

I saw in the waters merry,
  Dear faces of long ago,
That had drifted away on the sea of life,
  As the winds blew loud or low.

My brain grew dazed with horror,
  And my heart was wrung with pain ;
Some barks were dashed on a rock-bound coast.
  They could not return again.

I saw the same old mill-pond,
   And beside it the noisy mill,
And once again I heard the bell
   Of the old Church on the hill.

There was the dear old School-House,
   The scene of my childhood joys,
And in the yard I romped among
   The happy girls and boys.

And once again came "May Day,"
   When the fields were dressed in green,
And roses shed their rich perfume,
   The children crowned me Queen.

I saw again our own sweet home
   Half hidden 'mong the trees,
My parents, brothers, sisters and I,
   As happy and busy as bees.

Around the door of the homestead,
   The sweet Wistaria vines,
And on the old oak in the yard
   The clinging ivy twines.

There stands the grim old court-house,
   And the Jail with dingy cells,
And on the Church the old town-clock
   The fleeting moment tells.

Next I came to the old town Graveyard
   And entered with silent tread,
And dropped a tear o'er the grassy grave
   Of the peacefully sleeping dead.

TO WHITTIER.

I N childhood's sunny day my heart was taught to love
   Thy name, all other poet's names above,
And when to womanhood at last I came,
Behold the spark was fanned into a flame,
Nor did I dare presume that I should live,
And to the honored, white-haired poet give
My sentiment in rude constructed rhyme;
O, wondrous change wrought by the hand of time!

When he who came the slaves among to dwell,
From frigid Idaho (we loved him well,)
Athirst for knowledge I stood at his side,
With quickening thought and eyes astonished, wide.
He nightly read, and held me on his knee,
From Whittier's " Snowbound" filling me with glee.
The seed sown by his hand in infant heart,
Has lived and grown, and cannot now depart.

Now to the sunset thou hast set thy face,
And silvery crown thy head doth grace;
The mind of fertile thought doth not decline
Preserved yet from the ravages of time
Since I can never hope my first desire,
To shake thy hand, which would my soul inspire,
Now e're yet "the cord is loosed or pitcher broken,"
Grant me with thine own hand this little token:
Ere yet that hand by feebleness grows lame,
With condescension write for me thy name.

WELCOME TO HON. FREDERICK DOUGLASS.

MT. ZION CHURCH, MARCH 5th. 1888.

OUR hearts are filled with pride to-day—
   We hail thee, Noble Sire,
Stern prejudice is swept away
   By Freedom's cleansing fire.

And o'er this Southland you may roam,
   With ne'er a cause to fear—
We bid thee WELCOME to our home,
   Welcome, and right good cheer!

From rugged Blue Ridge mountain peak,
   To ocean's white crest wave :
Even infant lips thy praises speak,
   And boast thy deeds so brave.

The bondsman's fetters long since broke
   And tossed aside by thee,
Thou hurledst off the *cursed* yoke,
   And panted to be free.

We see thee in thy cradle-bed,
   Thy mother's pride and joy;
When from oppression's hand you fled,
   When but a strippling boy.

Thou, Moses of the negro race,
   This day we hail with pride;
The day that brings us face to face,
   And Douglass by our side.

From the feast of reason and flow of soul,
   And walls resounding with glee;
From the crimson goblet and flowing bowl,
   Is he giving one thought to me?

Ah! yes, on the wings of the night breeze come
   Such tidings of comfort to me.
Rest well, little Queen! his heart is thy throne,
   Who sends this message to thee:
" Thou need'st not fear, though in gilded halls,
   Of pleasure and chivalry,
Thy lover would'st fly from the mirthful walls,
   To spend one sweet moment with thee."

Yes, he thinks of me in the crowded mart,
   And the thought cheers him on his way;
I read in his eyes the desire of his heart,
   As he passes me day by day.
What more could I ask, what wish while I live,
   Than the love he has lavished so free?
This world has no worthier boon to give,
   Than my handsome young lover to me.

FAREWELL TO ALLEN UNIVERSITY.

"CLASS SONG OF '87."

" Tune America."

WE leave thy courts to-day,
    Joyful has been our stay,
      Within thy walls.
Hence lie our paths apart,
    Tears will unbidden start,
While we with aching heart
    Shall leave thy halls.

'Twas here our wont to meet,
    Fondly each other greet,
      Each rising day.
United prayers ascend
    For Teacher, Parent, Friend,
And joyful notes would blend
    In tuneful lay.

Bright may thy glories shine,
    On all who at thy shrine,
      Will meekly stay.
Loudly, thy praises tell!
    Loud Hallelujahs swell!
While we on earth shall dwell,
    We homage pay.

Dear " Allen," now to you,
    Classmates and Teachers, too.
      Farewell is said.
Still on that brighter shore,
    When all life's cares are o'er,
We'll meet and part no more,
    With Christ our head.

NIGHT.

———

THE shades of eve are quickly closing in,
   And streaks of silver gild the eastern sky,
Belated songsters have their vespers sung
   With happy hearts and silvery noted tongue,
The busy world has ceased its toil and din,
   And guardian angels now their watch begin.

All nature quiet save the sighing wind,
   And distant murmur of the ocean wave,
Which seem engaged a requiem to sing
   O'er blighted hopes and expectations grave.
The drooping heart its lonely vigil keeps,
   Beside the tomb where proud ambition sleeps.

But memory bids defiance unto sleep,
   And from her quiet chamber, see her creep,
Away she flies o'er hill, and dale, and mead,
   To find the Sacred City of the dead;
Faint not, nor stops to seek a rest,   [breast.
   Till pillowed on some loved and lost one's

THE PARTING.

THE die is cast, and we must part,
  Forgive me if I say we must;
Must make again exchange of heart,
  But never more exchange of trust.
With faces cold and stern must meet,
  While inward fires consume our souls,
Must pass as strangers in the street,
  While o'er our hope the death bell tolls.

We met but a short while ago,
  And all my sky was clouded o'er
You loved, and scattered all my woe,
  Loved as I ne'er was loved before.
You taught my hungry heart to hope,
  And filled love's chaliee to the brim,
But hope must now in darkness grope,
  And love s sweet sunshine e'er be dim.

When eventide has wrapped the world,
  In garments of a silvery sheen,
And diamond studded skies unfurled
  Their beauty fair to deck the Queen.
Of night, as she shall joyous ride
  In magic splendor on her way,
Like modest sweet and haypy bride,
  All glorious in her perfect sway.

My thoughts unfettered fly to thee,
  Untramelled by my heart's deep woe,
Though all our actions guarded be,
  Love's tender voice still murmurs low.

And fans the embers into flame,
   My heart thrills with its ecstacy
At any mention of thy name
   Forgets, and longs to be with thee.
Yet we must smile and kiss the rod,
   That strikes the blow and severs us,
Must fix our hope on heaven and God,
   Earth's joys are ever severed thus.
Farewell, and though we parted be,
   And parting brings us bitter pain,
Someday we shall united be,
   For we must hope to live again.

When all our wrongs have righted been,
   And crooked paths have been made straight,
When from our joy shall drop the screen,
   Which now is hung by cruel fate.
Then the full craving of each heart,
   Is granted, we shall happy be
When meeting we shall no more part,
   In the blissful realm eternity.

ASSURANCE.

I KNOW that his eyes look into mine,
   With a joy tongue cannot tell,
And I drink of the cup of love's sweet wine,
   And my heart says, "All is Well."
I know my heart is all my own,
   Enchained by love's sweet spell,
That I reign as a Queen on a golden throne,
   And my heart says all is well.

HOPE.

HOPE ! Thou vain, delusive maiden,
   Every moment cometh laden,
With some fresher, newer fancies,
   Which before our vision glances,
Filling hearts already burning
   With a deeper, stronger yearning;
Adding fuel to the fires,
   Waking all the soul's desires.
Nectar holdeth to our lip,
   Yet forbiddeth us a sip.

O, thou lovely, fickle jade,
   Fools of men hast ever made.
We thy fleeting footsteps follow,
   O'er the mountain in the hollow;
In the glade or through the dell
   Captives bound by thy sweet spell.
Tyrant Queen, what power is thine!
   Prince and Peasant at thy shrine,
For thy favor each imploring
   Through thy coquettish alluring.

Pointing with thy finger gentle
   To fair Fame's or Croesus' temple,
On thou leadest ever smiling
   Over rugged roads beguiling.
Youth and maiden, sire and sage,
   All in thy mad flight engage;
There's a better name for thee—
   Disappointment it should be.

" FAME."

WHAT'S in a name ? What's in a name ?
　　Some Ancient writers ask.
In truth to tell what's in a name,
　　We find no easy task;
Yet each and every noble deed
　　Helps build the house of fame;
And upon every block of stone,
　　We carve some Hero's name.
So let us live, while life is spared,
　　In duty's sunshine fair,
Our names shall be like temples reared ;
　　Not "Castles in the Air."

" TRUTH."

LOOK up, dear one, nor be cast down,
　　For bright again will shine thy sun,
God's smiles are hid behind his frown—
　　Trust Him, He will dispel thy gloom.

For T. M. D. W.

SUNSHINE AFTER CLOUD.

———

COME, "Will," let's be good friends again,
　　Our wrongs let's be forgetting,
For words bring only useless pain,
　　So wherefore then be fretting.

Let's lay aside imagined wrongs,
　　And ne'er give way to grieving,
Life should be filled with joyous songs,
　　No time left for deceiving.

I'll try and not give way to wrath,
　　Nor be so often crying ;
There must some thorns be in our path,
　　Let's move them now by trying.

How, like a foolish pair were we,
　　To fume about a letter;
Time is so precious, you and me;
　　Must spend ours doing better.

SLUMBERING PASSION.

———

CAN it be true, that we can meet,
  As other strangers in the street;
No deep emotions quickly rise,
  No hidden language in our eyes,
No sudden crimson-mantled cheek,
  No thrilling word of pleasure speak ?

Yes ! Thine was love of yesterday;
  This morning found it far away,
In search of newer conquests gone,
  Leaving me desolate and lone,
In vain I sought to break the spell,
  My strenuous efforts fruitless fell.

The cloud o'erspread my sunny sky,
  And settled slowly like a pall,
And clad my life in misery,
  And swept it clear of pleasures all,
Remembrance brings me only pain,
  My love, my truest love lies slain.

Henceforth in loneliness I grope
  My way, until my life shall end;
Among the hopeful, without hope,
  Among the friendly without friend—
My heart unto its depth is shaken,
  My love, untiring love forsaken.

THE ADVANCE OF EDUCATION.

WHAT means this host advancing,
  With such melodious strain:
These men on steeds a prancing,
  This mighty marshaled train.

They come while drum and fife resound,
  And steeds with foam aflecked,
Whose restless feet do spurn the ground,
  Their riders gaily decked.

With banners proudly waving,
  Fearless in Freedom's land,
All opposition braving,
  With courage bold they stand.

Come join the raging battle,
  Come join the glorious fray;
Come spite of bullets' rattle,
  This is enlistment day.

Hark ! hear the Proclamation
  Extend o'er all the land;
Come every Tribe and Nation
  Join education's band.

Now the command is given—
  Srike ! str*i*ke grim ignorance low;
Strike till her power is riven;
  Strike a decisive blow.

MOTHER.

WHO was it who held me on her knee ?
When I was helpless as could be,
And hoped such noble things of me ?
> My Mother.

Who taught my infant lips to prat,
And understood my childish chat,
And who in patience calmly sat ?
> My Mother.

Who watched me grow from day to day,
Taught me "Our Father's prayer" to say,
And keep me out of evil's way.
> My Mother.

Who shared my sorrow and my grief,
And always brought me sweet relief ;
Of all my friends who is the chief?
> My Mother.

Who always wisest council gave,
And taught me how life's storm to brave,
That I might safely ride each wave?
> My Mother.

Who guarded me from tempter's snare
Made me the burden of her prayer,
And watched with zealous tender care?
> My Mother.

And when the sun sinks in the west,
And birds fly homeward to their nest,
On whose fond bosom would I rest?
> My Mothers.

THE OUTCAST.

WITH pinched cheeks hollow and wan,
   With feet all travel sore,
A form so fragile, that one might span
Her waist. There she peers in each door.
A dress, that is scarcely a dress at all—
No hat to protect her head;
The matted brown hair speaks woe and despair,
As daily she begs for bread.

No shoes to cover her feet,
No table with bounties spread,
No home but a stoop in a wretched street,
And naught but rags for a bed.
One glance at the hungry face,
One look at the shattered frame
Would prove that her life has been but a race
With poverty, hunger and shame.

The hurrying crowd swept by,
On business or pleasure intent—
No time to give heed to a cry of need,
No help to the beggar lent.
Oh! Men with purse-string tight,
And women of comfort and ease,
Have you no pity this bitter night,
Her hunger and want to appease?

She knelt on the flagstones in prayer,
With uplifted heart unto heaven;
A pitying angel discovered her there,
And whispered so kindly: " Forgiven!"
The morning's sun looked on the face,
Of her who had known naught but pain,
So peaceful in death, not even a trace
Of hunger and suffering remain.

THE EARTHQUAKE OF 1886.

WITH angry brow and stately tread,
　　This mighty Warrior came;
With thundering throat his forces led,
　　With breath almost flame.
And eyes of penetrating glance,
　　That pierce through every vein,
As soldier pierced by soldier's lance,
　　Earth groaned and writhed in pain.

The fearless eagle in nis nest
　　Upon the mountain's height,
Arose with wonder in his breast,
　　And quivered with affright.
Old ocean troubled in his bed,
　　At first the shores forsook—
Returning, all his furies led,
　　And crept into each nook.

Brave-hearted men like statues stood
　　Powerless to strike a blow;
Their homes became as kindling wood,
　　Their city's walls laid low.
While mothers clasped their babes in arms
　　And sped with panting breath;
With faces full of dread alarm,
　　They sought to fly from death.

Husband and wife in long embrace
　　In mutest wonder stood;
Each horror read in other's face,
　　And knelt and prayed to God.
Death reaped a harvest as he rode
　　On wings of every wind;
He slew the young, the brave and good.
　　And some grown old in sin.

The very stars their light refused
　　To witness scene like this;
Fair Lunar hid away confused,
　　And veiled herself in mist.
Roar after roar, peal after peal,
　　The fierce bombardment went,
'Till nature like a drunkard reeled,
　　Her strongest breastworks rent.

"Surrender!" comes from every lip;
　　"We yield," from every breast;
Ourselves of selfishness now stript,
　　We are humbled in the dust.
In meek humility we bowed
　　And smiling kissed the rod,
That while it smote us, bore us up
　　Near to the throne of God.

TO YOUTH.

HOW shall your name go down in History,
   In letters of gold, or enveloped in mystery;
In deeds of love, on pages of white,
   In defense of the wrong in lieu of right—
In a selfish way will you carve your name ?
   Time surely will answer: What's in a name?

The leaves of your life each day are unfolding
   Your deeds of to-day; to-morrow, beholding,
May tint your cheek with the blush of shame,
   While your heart will question: What's in a name ?
Will you gather the jewels spread out at your feet,
   Or still with the idle ones find a seat ?

No definite cause in the world pursuing—
   In the idle brain mischief is ever brewing—
Can you find no work in the market-place,
   Can you not with the horsemen contend in the race;
If the footmen outstrip you who is to blame ?
   Be careful in youth how you carve your name.

"ON GENESSARETT."

OUT, upon the deep old ocean,
  Out, upon the trackless wave,
Tossed by winds in fierce commotion—
  Men with hearts no longer brave—
Drifted a poor helpless vessel,
  Driven by the winds at will;
Struggling sailors with her wrestle,
  Lest they watery graves should fill.

All night long they toiled in rowing,
  Striving their frail bark to guide—
Morning's streaks were longer growing,
  Still she tossed from side to side.
Some were on the oars hard bending,
  Others strove to man the sail,
But each moment strength seemed lending,
  To the e'er increasing gale.

Silently each weary seaman,
  Did the task to him assigned;
Helpless starboard watch, and leamen
  Scanned the trackless waste behind.
Fainter grew their hearts within them,
  For the billows threatened death,
Furious breakers fought to win them,
  Prayers were uttered with each breath.

Denser grew the clouds above them,
  And the tempest wildly raged,
Weary Captain, hopeless seamen,
  Each in silent prayer engaged.

Sudden on the wave appearing,
  Breaks a strange mysterious light
Toward their little bark 'tis nearing,
  And they tremble with affright.

" 'Tis a spirit," said they lowly,
  Terror on their faces spread,
But he neared them, speaking slowly—
  " It is I!" be not afraid.
Peter spake, (the all-impulsive)
  Jesus come Thy people save,
If indeed thou art our Jesus,
  "Bid me walk upon the wave!"

" Come unto me!" said the Saviour;
  Peter made a noble start,
But ere long his strength forsook him—
  Doubting filled his faithless heart.
In his own strength he was thinking
  He would walk upon the wave—
Soon he found that he was sinking,
  Then he cried " Lord Jesus Save!"

Then the loving Saviour caught him,
  And unto the vessel came ;
Peace now reigned, and Jesus taught him,
  Not thy power, but Jesus' name.
Sinner you are on the ocean,
  Sinking now beneath the wave,
Stretch Thine arms with faith's devotion—
  Jesus Christ is quick to save!

HE COMES NOT TO-NIGHT.

MY eager waiting heart can bear no more—
 Hark ! was that not his knock upon the door,
Or, that his footstep on the casement floor?
 No, the clock rings out the hour, 'tis nine,
'Tis past his hour and dreary waiting's thine
 Sad heart, he will not come to-night.

With anxious eyes, the gloom I strive to pierce,
 The stars are hid and winds are howling fierce ;
Only the ticking of the clock I hear,
 No welcome footsteps greet my eager ear.
'Tis past his hour and hopeless waiting thine
 Sad heart ! He will not come to-night.

From nature's fount the crystal tear drops flow,
 They soothe the throbbing heart's cry low,
O, heart thine is the common, common fate,
 Thou yet must learn to hope and wait,
Tis long since past his hour, vain waiting thine
 Sad heart. He will not come to-night.

WELCOME HOME.

———

THY weary feet have pressed once more thy native soil,
  After the weeks and days of care and toil,
And loyal hearts whose friendship ever is true,
Have come to bid a Welcome Home to you.

Our bosoms swelling with an honest pride,
As swells the lover's heart who claims his bride,
With pleasure and with joy, we grasp thy hand
And bid thee welcome to thy native land.

Like silvery star that glint and gleams at night,
Gladdening the wanderer's heart who seeks the light,
Like France who turned to her Joan of Arc,
We follow thee to victory from the dark.

Even though the call was made from distant land,
"Come join us sisters of the Missionary Band."
The bugle sound fell on thy willing ear,
And to thy faithful bosom came no fear.

And waiting not to rate the fearful cost,
In duty's call absorbed, all else is lost;
Through heat or cold, where'er thy path hath led,
Thine energies were bent, thy footsteps sped.

Thy fearless heart that knew not how to falter,
Laid quick thine all on sacrificial altar,
The dear ones of thy heart, thy friends and home,
And dared to brave old ocean's turbid foam.

For thee, the much oppressed Hammitic race
May justly claim a worthy heroine's place,
With those whose courage ne'er was known to flank,
Place Fanny Jackson Coppin in the foremost rank.

And may thy noble deeds be told in verse and song,
To those unborn who shall our places throng,
When o'er our dust the weeping willow waves,
And we shall calmly sleep within our graves.

SABBATH BELLS.

(Tune, "What a Friend we have in Jesus.")

SWEET and calm the breezes stealing
O'er the quiet Sabbath day;
　　Loud and long the church bells pealing,
　　　Haste to worship, haste away.
List their notes of music swelling,
　　Hark, what tones of melody!
Man's redemption they are telling;
　　　Haste to worship, haste away.

Now the six days' labor ended—
　　Temporal duties laid aside,
With our hearts and voices blended,
　　In his courts to-day abide.
Since the holy law was broken
　　From his fold, we've gone astray,
But the pardoning word was spoken;
　　Erring one retrace thy way.

With the Father interceding
　　For a sin-accursed race,
Hands and feet and side all pleading,
　　Jesus saves us by his grace.
Sinners list the bells are ringing,
　　'Tis the gospel's precious sound;
Infant tongues his praises singing,
　　Come, and in his courts be found.

In his promise trusting, never,
  Backward cast thy longing eyes;
Upward, onward pressing ever,
  Till the final morn arise.

List, the bells are loudly calling,
  Will you heed the call to-day ?
On whose ear the sound is falling,
  Haste to worship, haste away.

THE DAY AFTER CONFERENCE.

HOW quiet and how still to-day old Bethel's corners
  'round,
No boisterous clash of voices, no noisy gravel sound ;
And those who came from Territory, Island or from State,
Who for the glorious cause of Christ came here to
    legislate,
Are gone—and over Bethel hangs a quiet-like a pall,
And yet there seems to linger strange whisperings in her
    wall.

Perhaps it's but the echo of the meeting that is o'er,
Or may be it's a gathering come from the heavenly shore;
Yet they are here and on each face there rests a sad-
    dened look,
As with their index finger they keep tally in a book.

They are gathering up the doings of the Conference that
    is past,
They are making up reports that through eternity shall
    last.

And upon their heavenly faces comes anon a look of shame
As with terrible precision they record each member's
    name.
O ! ministers of Jesus, have your deeds been foul or fair ?
If the roll were called in glory, could you guiltless answer
    there !
Could your soul in Jesus' presence, pure and clean and
    white appear,
Or should some foul stain on it condemn you to despair?

Shall your tongue shout glad hosannahs at the gathering
    in of sheaves,
Or shall you empty-handed go, no fruit, but only leaves?
Shall the Master's loving smile assign you to a mansion
    bright,
Or shall his angry voice appoint you to the realms of night?
Look well! for these committees shall report all by and by,
Before the Great Archbishop in the Conference in the sky.

THE QUARREL.

I SAW him yesterday,
　As he passed upon his way,
　　To and fro.
Not a single word he spake,
　Though his heart seemed fit to break;
　　With its woe.

I understand his look,
　Like the pages of a book;
　　Which I've read.
Oh ! however the heart may ache,
　Back the words we cannot take;
　　Now they're said.

How willingly I'd share
　Half the burden of his care;
　　If I might.
A word's a cruel thing,
　And how long we feel the sting;
　　Of a slight.

But I love him just the same;
　May be he's not all to blame;
　　Perhaps 'twas me.
And I've just received a note,
　Which with his own hand he wrote;
　　Let me see.

Oh ! he's coming here to-night,
And we'll set the matter right;
He'll explain.
And we'll love each other better,
For the mistake in the letter;
And the pain.

THOU LOVEST ME.

GRACIOUS Saviour let me make,
Neither error or mistake—
Let me in Thy love abide,
Ever near Thy riven side.

Let me, counting all things dross,
Find my glory in the cross ;
Let me daily with Thee talk,
In Thy footsteps daily walk.

I would gladly follow Thee,
For Thou gently leadest me,
Where the pastures green doth grow,
Where the waters stillest flow.

For me is Thy table spread,
And Thou doth anoint my head,
And my cup of joy o'erflows
In the presence of my foes.

GENERAL ROBERT SMALLS.

———

BEAUFORT, fair Beaufort, thou art a favored spot,
For fate saw fit to cast in thee a noble hero's lot;
And we congratulate ourselves as in his house we stand,
As welcome guests to one of the most noted in the land.

Whose heart is warm as Southern sun, and noble, true
  and brave,
With patriotic fire full and restless as the wave;
Whose zeal and candor unconcealed, constrained us to
  admire;
Infused new zeal within our hearts and led us to aspire.

And 'mid these grand and gothic walls quite leasurely we
  saunter,
We ask him to rehearse to us the story of the "Planter"—
How when the fighting hottest grew, and strong hearts
  were dismayed,
Up to the pilot-house he flew and quick the fears allayed.

And though the whistling shot and shell fell thick on
  every side,
His deeds of valor we will tell to Nations yet with pride,
To Afric's sons and daughters we'll leave it as no mystery,
But hand them down on blocks of stone, and they shall
  live in history.

With Touissant L' Ouverture and Crispus Attuck brave,
John Brown and Abram Lincoln, who died to free the
　　slave—
They, the nation's martyrs, and each loyal negro's walls
Should be adorned with portraits of these and Robert
　　Smalls.

ADMIRATION.

IN the wondrous light of a pair of brown eyes,
　　What language I read in the distance;
My soul is suddenly lost in surprise,
And can offer therefore no resistance.
An easy prey to the magic spell
I fall, and am helpless to rise;
No subtler power in fairy dell,
Than that in those thrilling brown eyes.

One moment they quietly rested on me;
The next they were wantonly straying;
And now they're swimming in ecstacy,
Unaware of the havoc they're playing.
Just now they are looking quite innocently—
A moment before wondrous wise.
I would I could fathom the depth of that sea,
In those thrilling mysterious dark eyes.

MY HUSBAND'S BIRTHDAY.

SO you've reached your thirty-eighth birthday,
And by many a varied road—
I see that your hair is a trifle gray,
But you've toiled with a heavy load—
Of life's care, and pain, and sorrow,
Upon your shoulders broad;
You have striven that each to-morrow,
Found you nearer to heaven and God.

What matter if age creepeth o'er you,
Your spirit is young, still and bold;
The path of duty before you
Is paved with the purest of gold.
Not such as the brow of a monarch would grace,
Eclipsing the costliest gem,
That is torn from that bosom of earth's embrace,
More precious than diadem.

Though many the changes your eyes have seen;
In these few fast fleeting years,
O'er the graves of loved ones (now grown green,)
You've shed many bitter tears.
On life's great sea your bark has tossed,
And adverse winds have blown,
And threatening clouds your skies have crossed,
Yet still the sun has shone.

Now down the stream of life you glide,
And steer toward setting sun—
May each day's close bring sweet repose,
As you think on the good you have done.

DECORATION DAY.

WE gather where the weeping willow waves;
  With flowers we will strew the grassy graves—
Who enter here must come with softest tread,
  In presence of the brave and valiant dead.

Come, noble sons of Union, daughters fair:
  A dirge is floating on the summer air
O'er the city freedom's ensign proudly waves,
  Come, shed a tear above the fallen braves!

Strains of weird music freight the noonday air,
  And veterans tread the highways here and there.
Where peacefully repose the fallen braves,
  The birds are chanting requiems o'er the graves.

No more is heard the cannon's crash and roar,
  Peace spreads her joyful wings from shore to shore
No more is heard the musket's shower like hail,
  And hushed and still the mother's piteous wail.

Loud let the drum and fife with music sound,
  Loud let their praise be echoed all around;
Let loyal heart and voice join in the sound;
  Let infant hands with roses strew the ground.

WHO IS MY NEIGHBOR?

WE had gathered for the love-feast on the time ap-
    pointed night,
And many came with hearts aflame and swords all bur-
    nished bright;
And other heavy laden ones who, toiling on life's road,
Forgot that Christ had promised to bear their heavy load,
Came struggling in the open door and dropped into a seat;
But failed to lay their burdens at the blessed Saviour's feet.

We sang the hymn "Redeeming Love," and then we knelt
    in prayer,
Not knowing that one steeped in sin had gathered with
    us there;
Then we arose and each in turn began of Christ to talk,
And some rejoiced and others moaned o'er life's intricate
    walk;
And when the Holy Spirit had pervaded every heart,
The weak grew strong, for all their doubts were bidden
    to depart.

We felt that faithful, earnest prayer would unlock heaven's
    door,
Lo, in our very midst, there stood a drunkard on the floor;
He'd wandered down the narrow street and stopped and
    made his bed
Upon the steps that to the very mercy-seat had led—
Where the thrilling songs of Zion and the atmosphere of
    prayer,
And the host of the invisibles floated on the evening air.

They roused him from his stupor, smote his conscience
    and his heart,
For he saw that with "the chosen" even here he had no
    part;
And struggling to control himself and decently appear—
He laid aside his tattered hat and to the desk drew near.
The muttered words stuck in his throat as hard he strove
    to speak:
"My friends, I've been a drinking," were uttered low
    and weak.

"Put the man out," they quickly cried, "how dare he
    interfere?
This is no place for drunkards, only the good are here."
And as the men advanced to take the poor intruder out,
He placed his hands behind him and despairing gazed
    about.
There rested such a look upon his now quite sobered face
Of hopelessness: it seemed to say they thrust me from this
    place.

Where prayers are made for erring ones, Christ says to
    all mankind:
"That whosoe'r believing comes shall full salvation find."
Strong hands were laid upon him and they led him to the
    door,
And from the church steps down he went perhaps to rise
    no more—
Who knows but a hasty step his lasting doom may seal,
Though sense of his unworthiness he yet may keenly feel.

Perhaps we, too, are erring, let us turn our eyes within;
Perhaps we'll have no trouble in discovering secret sin.
If the question were but answered how our cases stood
The echo of the answer would be: no, not one is good.
Let us be like Samaritans, and stoop when passing by,
To raise a fallen brother and to hear the needy's cry.

ETERNITY.

AWAY from earth and its cares set free,
    The soul in its blissful liberty
Shall soar to portals fair and bright;
Where sweet-voiced angels clad in white,
Are tuning their harps in heavenly glee:
    We hope to spend Eternity.

Over the crystal sea of glass,
And through the golden streets we'll pass,
Floating along on the placid streams;
Or roaming through fields of eternal green,
A glorious awakening there will be:
When we land on the banks of Eternity.

In that beautiful home so far away,
There come no nights of dark dismay;
The Saviour's love shall round us shine,
And light our steps through heavenly clime;
And while we join the sweet melody—
We'll rest throughout Eternity.

With faltering steps here, up and down,
With bleeding wounds from sole to crown,
We'll cast aside life's troubles here;
When, like the Saviour, we appear,
Sorrow and tears shall cease to be:
In our promised home in Eternity.

THE QUARTO CENTENNIAL.

O, THAT the Holy Angels would indite
   Fit words of praise that I might write;
Or to my timid faltering heart reveal,
Some secret hidden spring, some new found seal,
That guards a casket rich and rare and old,
Of gems as rich and pure as finest gold—
Or, to some unknown depth might I descend,
Or, would some fairy sprite its wings me lend,
That I might soar aloft and pierce the azure sky—
Might penetrate earth's bosom with discerning eye;
Or would the touch of heavenly hands inspire
My soul, then filled with pure and holy fire,
Might wake the cords that now lie dormant here,
And catch some rich vibrations from celestial sphere.

Year after year is born and glides away,
And generations rise and flourish and decay;
Flowers bud and blossom, fade and fall,
But the eternal truth outlives them all.
As in the forest stands the sturdy oak,

Where the young ravens scream and groan and croak,
Stand like monuments of the unhappy past,
Those who have brav'd the summer's heat, and
    winter's blast.

On mountain height where hungry eagles slept,
In deep ravine where poisonous reptiles crept,
Undaunted to the Master's call take they heed,
And proved themselves his followers indeed.

On, on, though often dark and chill the night,
In the vineyard gleaning with cycle bright,
In the rank marshes, or whereso'er He led,
The sky their only covering, the earth their only bed.

O, welcome day, when peace broods o'er the land;
Free and untrammeled roams the Christian band,
No guillotine is reared, no furious crackling stake;
No flames leap high the Christian's life to take.

How swift the flight of five and twenty years,
Freighted with hope and grief, with joy and tears;
To duty came the call that sacred day—
Strong in the Master's strength, Paul like they did
    obey.

But free to tread his own or foreign sod,
His voice upraised to the eternal God—
No bodies torn asunder fill untimely graves,
And o'er the world Salvation's Banner waves.

Oh ! Allen, you are with us here to-day,
Noting these services, this grand array;
Those sightless eyes methinks look into mine,
With holy happiness divine.

With gratitude we gather here and now—
Our praises render while we meekly bow
To heaven, who gave us such as thee,
And God's own Son who died to set us free.

HEART-HUNGRY.

O, Hungry Heart,
    Contend not with thy fate;
Lonely thou art,
    But yet must hope and wait.
For all thy craving,
    Thou shalt be filled;
Why this mad raving?
    Why so self-willed ?

Longing, art thou,
    For that which comes not?
Submissive bow,
    Sad is thy lot,
What must the end be ?
    Lest thou relent,
Love will consume thee,
    Thy power be spent.

Dost thy cold mate,
    That thou hast chosen
Smile at thy fate,
    With glances frozen.

O, hungry heart,
  In shadow groping
Still act thy part,
  And go on hoping?

Thy fate invites thee,
  Kind or unkindly;
Thou art not free,
  Love loves e'er bindly.
As thirsty meadow
  Welcomes the dew,
And as the shadow
  Follows the true.

All the emotion
  Thou dost impart,
Will find devotion,
  O, hungry heart.
O, hungry heart,
It is not in vain
  Somewhere, somehow!
For all thy pain.

  For all thy sorrow,
Thy bitter tears,
  Happiness borrow
From coming years.
  O, hungry heart,
Hope is all beauty,
Disappointment's dart
  Points thee to duty.

I WILL LOOK UP.

I WILL look up to Thee
   With faith's ne'er-failing sight,
My trust repose in Thee,
   Though dark and chill earth's night.

I will look up to Thee,
   Though rough and long the way,
Still sure Thou leadest me
   Unto the perfect day.

I will look up to Thee
   When lone and faint and weak.
" My grace sufficeth Thee;"
   I hear Thy soft voice speak.

I will look up to Thee,
   For if Thou, Lord, art near,
Temptations quickly flee,
   And clouds soon disappear.

I will look up to Thee
   With feeble voice I cry.
Lord, pity helpless me—
   Without Thy aid I die.

I will look up to Him
   Who died my soul to save;
Who boar my load of sin—
   His blood a ransom gave.

I will look up to Thee,
    The all-anointed one,
Who opes the gate for me,
    To the eternal throne.

I will look up to Thee;
    I feel my sins forgiven—
Thy footprints Lord I see,
    They mark the way to heaven.

I will look up to Thee,
    When doubt and fear arise;
Though dangers compass me,
    Upward I lift mine eyes.

I will look up to Thee,
    Who knoweth all my needs;
Thy spirit Lord grant me,
    My soul in anguish leads.

I will look up to Thee!
    Though all I have below,
Thou takest Lord from me,
    Thou canst the more bestow.

I will look up to Thee,
    Thou bright and morning star ;
With eyes of faith I see,
    Thy glory from afar.

I will look up to Thee,
    My hand shall rest in thine;
Where e'er thou wilt lead me,
    Thy will, O Lord, not mine !

I will look up to Thee,
　　When death's relentless hand,
Has laid it's weight on me,
　　Save—Thou atoning Lamb!

I will look up to Thee,
　　When crossing Jordan's wave;
Then Lord, I look to Thee—
　　Whose power alone can save !

HOPE THOU IN GOD.
—

O soul, why shouldst thou downcast be?
　　Or mourn thy temporal lot ;
Where'er 'tis cast, what's that to thee—
　　Doth not God choose the spot ?
Rouse thee, and labor for success!
　　And be thou well assured;
The shadows near the end grow less,
　　And pain must be endured.

Although I meet with conflicts here,
　　And storms beset my path,
Though devils shoot their fiery darts
　　Of disappointed wrath,
My feet upon the blood-marked way,
　　Shall ever onward press,
And looking to the " perfect day,"
　　My faith shall not grow less.

What if the ungodly spread a snare,
  And wicked councils·meet—
Lord, guard with loving, watchful care,
  My timid, faltering feet.
Soul, thou must daily suppliance make,
  If thou wouldst well be fed—
The righteous He will not forsake,
  Nor shall his seed beg bread.

The cloudy pillar day by day,
  The fiery cloud by night,
Shall mark the straight and narrow path,
  That leads to lasting light.
Where trembling hope receives her sight,
  Where flowers eternal grow—
God's presence beams forever bright,
  And living waters flow.

TO CLEMENTS' FERRY.

ONE lovely summer afternoon when balmy breezes blew,
A charming little buggy, scarce large enough for two,
Dashed down the narrow little street and stopped beside
a gate,
Where a charming little woman dwelt whom he had met
of late.

Out stepped a little body, looking like a happy bride ;
He gently stood and placed her in a safe seat at his side:
"I'm going to show you now," said he, (with eyes that
twinkle merry,)
" The very prettiest of drives, it leads to Clements'
Ferry."

" If you have never heard of it, my darling little treasure,
I'll tell you all about the place, it will afford me pleasure."
And on they sped, mile after mile, with chat and laughter
merry—
He watched her dimpled, roguish smile and drove toward
the ferry.

Through lovely groves, where birds sang sweet their notes
of joy so merry,
Or partridge, hid in ripened wheat, whistled his " Bob
White" cherry.
Up the shell road and o'er the fields and by the moss-
hung oaks,
Where marshy land its rich grain yields or sad-voiced
raven croaks.

Then turning off the highway and past the gate of toll,
Then up into a by-way which led straight to the knoll,
" 'Tis here, said he "the loveliest spot in all the world so
    wide,
Swept by the breezes from the sea, and kissed by every
    tide.

Come down beside the river's brink, where the water rip-
    ples merry—
A lovely place to rest and think, down here beside the
    ferry.
So taking his uplifted hands she gave a little bound,
And very soon they sat them down upon the grassy ground.

In days that are forever fled, when slavery cursed this
    nation—
This land was owned by "Clements" and on his great
    plantation
Were many slaves who daily tilled this soil, tho' oft in
    pain—
Their master's coffers must be filled from the fields of
    golden grain.

They knew no rest who labored there, but worked from
    early light—
They ploughed and hoed and reaped and sowed, till the
    sun went down at night ;
Then to the river they would come all foot-sore, worn
    and weary,
Hungry and faint to reach their home they crossed here
    at the ferry.

One day they heard a strange sweet voice, not such as
    won't to lead them;
It made their burdened hearts rejoice, for 'twas the voice
    that freed them.
And when the sun went down that night their shouts rose
    loud and merry—
They crossed with footsteps swift and light the last time
    o'er this ferry.

"So here besides this river we have found a rustic seat,
And still the water rippled on and winds blew soft and
    sweet—
"I've something else to tell you," and his laughing eye
    were merry,
He whispered something in her ear, but not about the
    ferry.

    *   *   *   *   *   *

The sun was shining in the west and back toward home
    they drove;
Soft twilight had its shadows cast o'er field and "knoll"
    and grove—
The "ferry has another name, which lovers oft repeat,
Instead of "Clements' Ferry," it is now "Sunset Retreat."

THE BIRTH OF TIME.

———

HAPPY moments tell me, pray,
  Where were you on yesterday ?
While I sit, bowed low with sorrow,
Tell me where you'll be to-morrow.

Come you from a heavenly clime,
Linger with me all the time ;
Every day will then be bright,
Every burden then seem light.

Are you slumbering with the flowers,
While I have my darkest hours ?
I am sure it would be pleasant
If I found you ever present.

Happy moments seemed to say :
"I am busy all the day;
Every hour I well must fill,
So I never can be still.

You, my friend, would happier be,
If you busy kept like me ;
Then your joys would seem the sweeter,
And your dark hours would seem fleeter.

More of joy and less of grief,
All your days of labor brief,
If the moments you improve,
By some little deed of love.

All the earth is full of beauty,
Where we live and do our duty;
Then your sun will seem the brighter,
And your heavy heart grow lighter.

May I ask you, idle one,
To recount the good you've done,
To deserve the joys you've tasted—
Now account for time you've wasted!"

Then I felt a sudden start,
And the impulse of my heart
Was, that I must work to-day;
For the moments haste away.

Little moments, will you wait
While your wings with prayer I freight;
So when I drop out of time,
I may see God's smile divine?

I could not a moment borrow,
For to-day is gone to-morrow;
And to-morrow is "to-day,"
So the debt I could not pay.

Tell me moments : whence your birth,
Whence your coming to the earth?
Was your birthplace 'mid the flowers,
Or in cloudless, fleece-like bowers?

Then the answer quickly came
Like a chipped-off lightning flame:
"When the great Creator flung
Out the world, on nothing hung,
Then was I destined to be,
Time until Eternity."

TENNYSON'S POEMS.

On receiving Tennyson's Poems from Mrs. M. H. Dunton, of Brattleboro', Vt.

DEAR Friend, since you have chosen to associate
  My humble thoughts with England's poet laureate,
I trust that he will bear me pleasant company,
And soon we shall far more than mere acquaintance be.
Since childhood's days his name I have revered,
And more and more it has become to me endeared;
I blush not for the truth, I but confess,
I very wealthy feel since I his "works" possess.

I've found in the immortal Shakespeare much delight,
Yet, oft his vulgar language shocked me quite;
And I twice grateful am, that I no more shall be
Dependent in spare moments on *his* company.
But I shall roam o'er England's proud domain,
Shall meet her lords and ladies, and her peasants
      plain,
Attend her royal spreads, and figure at her courts,
On prancing steed with nodding plume, I join their
      hunting sports.

THINE OWN.

TO live and not to be Thine Own,
  Like Springtime is when birds are flown;
Or liberty in prison bars,
Or evening skies without the stars;
Like diamonds that are lustreless,
Or rest when there's no weariness;
Like lovely flowers that have no scent,
Or music when the sound is spent.

LOVE LETTERS.

DEAR Letters, Fond Letters,
  Must I with you part?
You are such a source of joy
  To my lonely heart.

Sweet Letters, Dear Letters,
  What a tale you tell;
O, no power on earth can break
  This strange mystic spell!

Dear Letters, Fond Letters,
  You my secret know—
Don't you tell it, any one—
  Let it live and grow.

MATIN HYMN.

IS this the way my Father,
  That Thou wouldst have me go—
  Scaling the rugged mountain steep,
  Or through the valley low?
  Walking alone the path of life,
  With timid, faltering feet;
  Fighting with weak and failing heart,
  Each conflict that I meet?

Nay! nay! my child, the Father saith,
  Thou dost not walk alone—
  Gird up the loins of thy weak faith,
  And cease thy plaintive tone.
  Look thou with unbeclouded eyes
  To Calvary's gory scene—
  Canst thou forget the Saviour's cries?
  Go thou, on His mercy, lean.''

My Father, brighter grows the way,
  Less toilsome is the road;
  If Thou Thy countenance display,
  O, lighter seems my load!
  And trustingly I struggle on,
  Not murmuring o'er my task;
  The mists that gather soon are gone,
  When in Thy smile I bask.

Turn not from me Thy smiling face,
Lest I shall surely stray,
But in Thy loving arms' embrace,
I cannot lose my way.
My Father when my faith is small,
And doubting fills my heart,
Thy tender mercy I recall.
O, let it ne'er depart!

I LOVE THEE.

THOU art not near me, but I see Thine eyes,
Shine through the gloom like stars in winter skies—
Pointing the way my longing steps would go,
To come to Thee because I love Thee so.

Thou art not near me, but I feel Thine arm,
Soft folded round me, shielding me from harm,
Guiding me on as in the days of old—
Sometimes life seems so dark, so dreary and so cold.

Thou art not near me, but I hear Thee speak,
Sweet as the breath of June upon my cheek,
And as Thou speakest I forget my fears,
And all the darkness, and my lonely tears.

O love, my love, whatever our fate may be,
Close to Thy side, or never more with Thee,
Absent or present, near or far apart,
Thou hast my love and fillest all my heart.

MY CANARY.

LITTLE bird with tuneful throat,
   Happy heart and silvery note—
Dainty beak and feathers yellow,
   Thou art such a charming fellow.

Always merry, full of glee,
   Seeming happy as can be—
All the house with music thrilling,
   And my heart with pleasure filling.

Could I sing I'd vie with thee:
   In sweet strains of melody
We would raise our voices high,
   To praise our Maker in the sky.

MY MOCKING BIRD.

NO gorgeous coat has he,
   He is plain as he can be;
Singing all the live-long day,
   Imitating what I say.
Mocking ev'ry bird in bush,
   Sparrow, wren, or hawk or thrush,
Parrot, robin, finch or crow,
   Owl, oriole, bird of snow,
With cuteness quite astounding,
   Bird and man alike confounding.

MORN.

—

FRESH and fair the morn awaketh,
  From her couch of down;
Parting kiss her lover taketh,
  Ere his daily journey maketh
  Of the world around.

For a jolly-hearted rover,
  Ever full of fun,
Making calls the wide world over,
  Flower and leaf, and blade and clover,
  Welcome him, the sun.

Gloom from weary hearts dispelleth,
  Shedding joy and light
O'er the homes where sorrow dwelleth,
  Of eternal sunshine telleth,
  And the mansions bright.

Evening's gentle voice is pleading,
  But he will not stay;
Her entreaties all unheeding,
  Morning's tender smile succeeding,
  Beckons him away.

Now while just a halo lingers,
  Note his roguish smile;
With the tip ends of his fingers,
  Sweet good day he gently flings her,
  But retreats the while.

DO YOU THINK?

DO you think, when you plan for to-morrow,
　　That the morrow you may not see,
　　That long ere the dawn of the morrow's morn,
　　　You may be in eternity.

Do you tread in the foot-steps of Jesus,
　　In the darkness as well as the light ?
Should the death angel come, to summons you
　　　home—
　　Say, would it be glory, or night ?

MUSIC.

O, wondrous depth to which my soul is stirr'd,
　　By some low tone, some softly breathed word—
Some thrill or cadence sweet which fills my heart,
　　My inmost powers wake, and thrill and start.
My bosom seems too narrow a confine,
　　For such a power, dear music as thine.

O, that my heavy, heavy falt'ring tongue,
　　Could warble forth thy ev'ry prompted song,
The world should join the gladsome song I'd raise,
　　And to the King shout lofty notes of praise.

E'en when my heart is wrapt in sorrow's night,
   Mine eyes of clay are clos'd, but heavenly light
Doth shine into the desert of my soul,
   And billows of sweet music o'er me roll.

A MOTHER'S LOVE.

WHAT sacrifice so great !
   No hour too early, or too late,
No isle too distant, no shore or strand,
   She may not reach with earnest heart, and will-
        ing hand.

What love so strong !
   It is her child, or right or wrong,
In crowded court of justice, if condemn'd,
   Her love and tearful eyes doth still defend.

What love so pure !
   Friendship oft is false, but one is sure,
That mother's love clings to us to the last,
   Wherever in life our varied lot is cast.

MY GRACE IS SUFFICIENT.

———

IS thy sun obscured to-day,
  By a cloud of sorrow?
It cannot be thus alway,
  Bright may be the morrow.
Hast thou left of hope a spark?
  Sit not down repining—
Never was there cloud so dark,
  Had not silver lining.

Adverse currents strong and swift
  Sweep across thy soul—
Courage, heart, the cloud must rift,
  It will backward roll.
Is thy bark far from the land,
  On a tempestuous ocean?
Stretch to God thy helpless hand,
  He can stay commotion.

Sits thy soul in grief to-day
  'Neath the weeping willow?
On the Son thy burden lay,
  Soft will seem thy pillow.
Doth amidst thy course arise
  Difficulty's, mountain;
Sweetest draught his love supplies
  From the crimson fountain.

Dost thou wander weak and faint,
　　Through life's desert lonely?
God regards the feeblest plaint,
　　He can aid thee only.
Without His all-seeing eye,
　　Not a sparrow falleth;
More He heeds the humble cry,
　　That for mercy calleth.

Raise to God thy streaming eyes,
　　Contrite heart's petition—
Let no waves of doubt arise,
　　For thy sad condition.

WHERE DO SCHOOL DAYS END ?

A LITTLE child sat on the floor,
　　Turning the pages o'er and o'er,
Of Mother Goose's nursery book;
He raised his eyes with puzzled look,
And said, "Mamma, attention lend,
And tell me: Where do school days end ?"

My boy, that is no easy task—
A weighty question 'tis you ask;
For every day adds to our store
Of knowledge gained the day before;
So you must ask some wiser friend
To tell you, where school days will end.

The parson came that very day,
His usual pastoral call to pay;
The child stole in with cunning look,
And on a stool his seat he took.
Sir, will you information lend,
And tell me, where school days will end ?

The parson with astonished air,
Pushed his fingers through his hair;
Little child I am much afraid,
That I can give but little aid;
But my best efforts I will lend,
To tell you, where school days will end.

There is a land of light you know,
Where all good people are to go—
Where little children rob'd in white,
Are ever happy in God's sight.
And when you die He'll angels send,
To take you where school days shall end.

THE BIRTH OF JESUS.

QUIETLY the world lay sleeping,
　　Save on fair Judean plain;
Faithful Shepherds watch were keeping,
Lest their tender flocks be slain.

Silently the snowy mantle
O'er the hill and vale was spread—
Emblem of seraphic pureness—
Carpet fit for angels' tread.

Lo, in eastern skies appearing,
Backward seems the night to roll;
The prophetic star is nearing,
Heaven opened as a scroll.

Then the heralds gladly singing,
Came to announce the Prince of Peace,
All the heavenly harps were ringing—
Praises chaunt and never cease.

Then a cloud of golden glory
Filled the air with heavenly mirth,
Angels sang the wondrous story,
When the Christ-child came to earth.

A HAPPY HEART.

GIVE me a Happy Heart and suasive tongue,
   That I may cheer the aged and the young;
     That I may charm the little child,
       And make the winds of age seem mild.

Give me the willing hand and ready feet,
   To raise the brother lying in the street;
Give me the honest heart that has no fear,
   That with the humble I may shed a tear.

Give me the eye of faith that I may see
   Some good accomplished daily Lord for Thee—
Give me a heart full of Thy holy zeal,
   That I my neighbors joy or woe may feel.

Give me the feet that eagerly will run,
   About the Master's work, until the sun
Has faded in its glory in the west,
   And all the busy world has sought its rest.

WHEN I WOULD DIE!

NOT when leaves are brown and sere,
   Not when days are cold and drear;
   Not when roses faded lie,
   Not when clouds o'ercast the sky.
   But when spring-time breezes blow,
   And make sweet music, soft and low;
   When birds their happy carols sing,
   When flowers their lovely odors bring—
   When woods their richest verdure yield,

When lambs frisk in the clover-field;
When bee and butterfly fill the air,
When morn awaketh bright and fair;
When love upon the breeze is born—
Oh, I would die on Easter morn!

When the morn with lovely grace
Greets the world in soft embrace;
When the lily's rich perfume
Woos the minstrel's harp to tune,
And the lark his song of praises
To the Great Creator raises.
Upward soars in happy mood,
Loud his notes of gratitude,
For security and rest,
For the birdlings in his nest.
When the daisies dot the lawn,
I would die at Easter dawn!

When the year is blithe and young,
Happiness on every tongue—
After winter's icy chains
Lose their hold upon the plains;
When the waters, rippling on,
Tell the power of winter gone—
Spring leads him her willing slave,
Then lay me in the quiet grave;
Loved ones do not come and weep,
For I shall only be asleep;
Roses heap upon the mound,
And I shall rest both sweet and sound.
Let no heart for me be aching,
Christ will see to my awaking.

DECEMBER.

THE skies o'ercast and fierce winds blow,
    Their chilling breath thro' leafless trees,
    Streams fetter-bound in icy chains,
    And frosty net-work on the panes.
    The birds have sought a summer clime,
    Each tender floweret, bud and vine,
    Has hid away with timid fear,
    For lo, December days are here !
    The blazing logs are heard to crack,
    And all the grain is garnered now.

JUDGE NOT.

PERCHANCE, the friend who cheered thy early years,
    Has yielded to the tempter's power;
    Yet, why shrink back and draw away thy skirt,
    As though her very touch would do thee hurt ?
        Wilt thou prove stronger in temptation's hour ?

Perchance the one thou trusteth more than life,
    Has broken love's most sacred vow:
    Yet judge him not—the victor in life's strife,
    Is he who beareth best the burden of life,
        And leaveth God to judge, nor questions how.

Sing the great song of love to all, and not
    The wailing anthems of thy woes;
    So live thy life that thou may'st never feel
    Afraid to say, as at His throne you kneel,
        "Forgive me God, as I forgive my foes!"

UNUTTERED PRAYER.

—

MY God, sometimes I cannot pray,
  Nor can I tell why thus I weep;
The words my heart has framed I cannot say,
  Behold me prostrate at Thy feet.

Thou understandest all my woe;
  Thou knows't the craving of my soul—
Thine eye beholdeth whereso'er I go;
  Thou can'st this wounded heart make whole.

And oh ! while prostrate here I lie,
  And groan the words I fain would speak:
Unworthy though I be, pass not me by,
  But let Thy love in showers break.

And deluge all my thirsty soul,
  And lay my proud ambition low ;
So while time's billows o'er me roll,
  I shall be washed as white as snow.

Thou wilt not quench the smoking flax,
  Nor wilt thou break the bruised reed;
Like potter's clay, or molten wax,
  Mould me to suit Thy will indeed.

WHOSO GIVES FREELY, SHALL FREELY RECEIVE!

WHEN Jesus was leaving this sin-accursed land,
These words full of comfort he left with his band:
"Ye are not forsaken, my peace I will leave,
And whoso gives freely, shall freely receive!"

"Your Father in heaven, so righteous and just,
Will comfort your hearts, if in Him ye trust;
If only on Jesus, his Son, ye believe;
Then ye who give freely, shall freely receive!"

"On the just and the unjust descendeth the rain—
The fields all revived bring abundance of grain;
Give honor and glory and firmly believe,
That whoso gives freely, shall freely receive."

Step out from your door on a bleak winter day—
Half-clad and half-starving, you meet on your way,
Some one who is begging for alms to relieve.
Think! whoso gives freely, shall freely receive!

Perhaps but a penny dropped into a hat—
Yet the angel recording will take note of that.
Like the mite of the widow, whatever you give,
Much or little—give freely, you'll freely receive!

There are often around us dear souls in distress,
Who are needing not money, but kind words to bless—
Their lives seem so weary—a word will relieve;
Let's give to them freely, they'll gladly receive!

When finished our course in this vale here below,
When Christ shall the robe and the crown bestow
On those, who were faithful and quick to believe:
Who gave him their service shall freely receive!

WILBERFORCE.

Read at the 25th Anniversary of Wilberforce, Ohio, June, 1887.

A quarter century ago,
  A March morning, bleak and wild,
The joyful news spread to and fro:
To Afro Methodist is born a child;
Begotten in the time of strife,
And born in adverse circumstances,
All trembled for the young child's life,
It seemed to have so poor a chance.
But, nursed by every care,
It stronger grew, until at last
Our hearts no longer feel a fear,
The danger is forever past.
The feeble childhood's days are flown,
How swiftly speed the years away;
We hail thee now a woman grown
In regal robes and Queen's array.

Thou dark-browed beauty of the west,
Thy matchless grace is widely known;
Rich jewels sparkle on thy breast,
Thy head supports a royal crown.
And through thy veins pure Afric's blood
Flows fearlessly along its course;
Thy cheeks are mantled by the flood;
We hail thee, lovely *Wilberforce !*

Thy palace gates are open wide—
All are invited to the feast;
From frigid North or Southern side,
From every point, from West to East.
Thou holdest in thine outstretched hand
The richest, rarest gifts to youth;
From snow-capped peak to ocean strand,
Thou offerest all the words of truth.

They come! their burning thirst, quench,
For wisdom, honor, knowledge, power;
From hidden depths rich jewels wrench—
Successful effort crowns each hour.
But foul incendiary's cruel hand,
Thy Territory did invade;
By ruthless and destructive brand,
Thy lonely walls were lowly laid.

When night had hushed the birds to sleep,
Out of his covert see him creep;
The crackling flame and lurid glare,
Burst out upon the midnight air.
And what had seemed so strong and fair,
Now lay a mass of ruins there;
Triumphantly look'd all our foes,
And gloated o'er our many woes.

But men of iron nerve and will,
Looked up to God, with courage still:
Believing He their cries would heed,
And prove a friend in time of need.

The tiny seeds of kindness sown,
Into a mighty tree has grown,
And youth and maiden side by side,
Sit 'neath its spreading branches wide.

And though the seed be sown in Payne,
The trite old saying we maintain:
That whosoe'er in Payne we sow,
By faith's tears watered it shall grow.
Our trust untarnished by alloy,
We sow in tears but reap in joy;
And may thy praises never cease,
And all thy paths be those of peace.

EASTER MORN.

LO ! the glorious dawn is breaking,
    And the night of gloom is gone,
All the earth from slumber waking,
    Hails with joy the Easter Morn!

Lo! the sun's bright rays are peeping
    Over Calvary's crimson height,
Soldier guards who watch were keeping,
    Saw Him rise in power and might!

Mary ran with footsteps fleeter,
 Than the other two who went—
Where an angel sat to greet her,
 And the grave a glory lent.

With their spices they were going,
 To the tomb where Jesus lay—
Faithful ones, without the knowing.
 Who should roll the stone away?

To the rich man's new sepulchre,
 Mary's eager feet drew near;
Lo, she saw the tomb was open,
 And her heart was filled with fear!

At the grave she stooped, and peeping,
 Angels saw in white arrayed,
Where her Lord was lately sleeping,
 "And the clothes aside were laid!"

Back she drew with fear and quaking,
 But the angel watcher said:
" Jesus is among the living,
 Seek Him not among the dead."

" He is risen, He is risen,"
 Now dispel thy gloom and fear
From the grave's embrace and prison;
 Rose triumphant, He is not here!

Then awake the song of gladness,
 Let it float upon the air.;
Joy dispels the gloom and sadness,
 Past the night of dark despair.

Shout with gladdest acclamation,
    Raise with joy the gladsome sound,
And with great acceleration,
    Spread to earth's remotest bound.

He is risen! great in glory;
    Death is vanquished, lost its sting !
Vain the grave can boast of victory,
    He is risen, Christ the King!

THE CITY BY THE SEA.

L OVE thee ? Yes, I'm sure I love thee,
    Dear old city by the sea;
Love thy grandly towering spires,
Love thy matrons and thy sires;
Love thy gallant sons so true,
Love thy genial skies of blue;
Love thy gentle fair-haired daughters;
And the music of thy waters
Flowing gently all around thee.
All are ever dear to me!

Hark ! I think I hear the echo,
Of the notes of melody;
And the chimes ecstatic pealing
From St. Michael's o'er me stealing,

Woos me back to pleasant hours
Spent among the fragrant flowers,
And the ocean's distant roar,
Bursts in music on the shore—
And the snowy white-capped waves,
Every nook and cranny laves,
As they break in sportive glee,
On the "battery" by the sea!

Of thy fame and vanished glory,
Dear old city by the sea—
All too well I know the story,
When thy deeds where dark and gory.
But the Inchcape bell's low moaning,
Echoes not the sad slave's groaning,
As from Afric's torrid sands,
He was brought in iron bands,
Writhing in his agony,
To the city by the sea!

Through the evening's mellow haze,
Dear old city by the sea,
What a picture meets my gaze,
Relic of departed days !
Standing yet the wave-washed Fort,*
From whose walls the loud report
Echoed all around the world—
(Now with stars and stripes unfurled)
Echoed like a bolt of thunder,
Burst the iron bands asunder,
Set the slave at liberty,
In the city by the sea!

*Sumpter

O'er thee broods the calm of peace,
Dear old city by the sea—
"Monitor," and "Ironsides,"
At thy port no longer ride.
But I would forget the past,
Lest a shadow it should cast
O'er my musing sweet of thee,
Dear old city by the sea!
And I love thee, still I love thee,
Ever dear art thou to me!

FORGETFULNESS !

"Darling," he said, "I never meant
　　To hurt you. "And his eyes were wet—
"I would not hurt *you* for the world;
　　Am I to blame, if I forget?"

"Forgive my selfish tears," she cried:
　　"Forgive! I knew that it was not
Because you meant to hurt me, sweet,
　　I knew it was that you FORGOT!"

But all the same, deep in her heart,
　　Rankled this thought, and rankles yet—
When love is at its best, one loves
　　So much, that one CANNOT FORGET!

THE NEW ORGAN.

Read at the Dedication of the New Organ at Mt. Zion Church,
Charleston, S. C.

THOU monstrous gilt and rainbow-tinted thing,
With many a thousand mouthed tuneful throat,
Helps us God's praises here to-day to sing,
With happy hearts we raise our joyful note.

What charms thou show'st to our uplifted gaze,
Some mystic hand seems now to lend thee power,
That fillest us with wonder and praise,
And mute we stand and tremble and adore.

Thou seems't almost human in thy tones;
Even he who built thee did not understand—
Sometimes low, plaint:ve, then so mirthful,
That thou wert peopled by an angel band.

O, tell us in thy strong, yet sweetest strain,
That He who died, now liveth evermore;
Yea thunder forth the sweet, ah! sweet refrain,
That Christ has left for men ajar the door.

And tell, forevermore, "Salvation's free,"
And pardon come to whosoever will,
Turn quick away from guilt and misery;
This pardon comes the hungry soul to fill.

And on the very air shall praises float,
While cherubim and seraphim shall sing;
And earth shall raise her very highest note,
While heaven, with loudest note, Alleluias ring!

When earth is wrecked and matter all consumed,
And all our labor here hath found an end,
Our happy souls shall strike harps, heavenly tuned—
Our voices with angelic voices blend.

So we shall praise Him while He lends us breath,
On viol, timbrel, lute, and harp and strings,
And when our mortal tongues are still in death,
Our praise shall mount on high on music's wings.

DECEPTION.

LIFE we find is nevermore
What at first we thought;
When deceit beclouds it o'er,
Sad the change that's wrought.

Confidence with drooping heart
Sadly takes its flight;
Fondest love will sure depart—
Day seems dark as night.

All the love of tender years
Turns to bitter hate;
Though repentance comes with tears,
It may be " too late"—

Though the heart in anguish yearn,
　　Lay in sackcloth low;
Confidence will not return,
　　Shattered by a blow.

Then while you possess it whole,
　　Strive it to retain;
Heart of truth and purpose, soul
　　Cannot cause you pain.

May the tender power of love
　　Penetrate your life—
True as are the stars above,
　　And as free from strife.

What a tangled web we weave;
　　What a chain of sorrow!
When we practice to deceive,
　　Gloom comes with the morrow.

OUT IN THE DESERT.

OUT in the desert afar, dost thou roam—
　　Out on the waste bleak and wild;
Why dost thou wander so far from thy home?
Wolves will o'ertake thee dear child.
　　Jesus stands pleading,
　　With wounds afresh bleeding;
O, come to his arms, meek and mild!

Out on the mountain so bare and so cold,
Hunger will blast thy fair cheek;
Jesus, the shepherd, has left the dear fold,
Now for THEE lost one to seek.
    Eventide falleth,
    His tender voice calleth—
Hear the sweet tones low and meek!

Wander no longer across the wild moor;
Back to the fold quickly flee!
Jesus has kindly left open the door—
Open, O, wanderer for thee!
    The light is still burning,
    He waits thy returning—
O, prodigal wander no more!

THE BLACK SAMPSON.

THERE'S a Sampson lying, sleeping in the land,
   He shall soon awake, and with avenging hand,
In an all unlooked for hour,
He will rise in mighty power;
   What dastard can his righteous rage withstand?

E'er since the chains were riven at a stroke,
E'er since the dawn of Freedom's morning broke,
He has groaned, but scarcely uttered,
While his patient tongue ne'r muttered,
   Though in agony he bore the galling yoke.

O, what cruelty and torture has he felt ?
Could his tears, the heart of his oppressor melt ?
In his gore they bathed their hands,
Organized and lawless bands—
   And the innocent was left in blood to welt.

The mighty God of Nations doth not sleep,
His piercing eye its faithful watch doth keep,
And well nigh His mercy's spent,
To the ungodly lent:
   "They have sowed the wind, the whirlwind they
      shall reap."

From His nostrils issues now the angry smoke,
And asunder bursts the all-oppressive yoke;
When the prejudicial heel
Shall be lifted, we shall feel,
   That the hellish spell surrounding us is broke.

The mills are grinding slowly, slowly on,
And till the very chaff itself is gone;
Our cries for justice louder,
'Till oppression's ground to powder—
   God speed the day of retribution on!

Fair Columbia's filmy garments all are stained;
In her courts is blinded justice rudely chained;
The black Sampson is awaking,
And his fetters fiercely breaking;
   By his mighty arm his rights shall be obtained!

"THEY ARE COMING?"

THEY are coming, coming slowly—
  They are coming, surely, surely—
   In each avenue you hear the steady tread.
From the depths of foul oppression,
Comes a swarthy-hued procession,
  And victory perches on their banners' head.

They are coming, coming slowly—
They are coming; yes, the lowly,
  No longer writhing in their servile bands.

From the rice fields and plantation
Comes a factor of the nation,
And threatening, like Banquo's ghost, it stands.

They are coming, coming proudly—
They are crying, crying loudly :
O, for justice from the rulers of the land !
And that justice will be given,
For the mighty God of heaven
Holds the balances of power in his hand.

Prayers have risen, risen, risen,
From the cotton fields and prison;
Though the overseer stood with lash in hand,
Groaned the overburdened heart;
Not a tear-drop dared to start—
But the Slaves' petition reach'd the glory-land.

They are coming, they are coming,
From away in tangled swamp,
Where the slimy reptile hid its poisonous head;
Through the long night and the day,
They have heard the bloodhounds' bey,
While the morass furnished them an humble bed.

They are coming, rising, rising,
And their progress is surprising,
By their brawny muscles earning daily bread;
Though their wages be a pittance,
Still each week a small remittance,
Builds a shelter for the weary toiling head.

They are coming, they are coming—
Listen ! You will hear the humming
Of the thousands that are falling into line:
There are Doctors, Lawyers, Preachers;
There are Sculptors, Poets, Teachers—
Men and women, who with honor yet shall shine.

They are coming, coming boldly,
Though the Nation greets them coldly;
They are coming from the hillside and the plain.
With their scars they tell the story
Of the canebrakes wet and gory,
Where their brothers' bones lie bleaching with
    the slain.

They are coming, coming singing,
Their Thanksgiving hymn is ringing.
For the clouds are slowly breaking now away,
And there comes a brighter dawning—
It is liberty's fair morning,
They are coming surely, coming, clear the way.

Yes, they come, their stepping's steady,
And their power is felt already—
God has heard the lowly cry of the oppressed :
And beneath his mighty frown,
Every wrong shall crumble down,
When the *right* shall triumph and the world be blest !

RT. REV. RICHARD ALLEN.

OUR RICHARD ALLEN in his early youth,
  Sought out and found the way of light and truth;
  His heart with holy impulse was stirred,
  And boldly forth he went to preach the word.

Sometimes he had not even a resting-place—
Footsore and weary, still he cried free grace;
And yet in pastures green the shepherd fed,
And by the cooling stream was often led.

Year after year is born and glides away;
Generations rise and flourish and decay;
Flowers bud and blossom, fade and fall,
But eternal truth outlives them all.

And so a hundred years have passed away,
Since the immortal ALLEN's natal day;
And where he sleeps the sun's departing ray
Long lingers, o'er that hallowed heap of clay.

He came of humble parentage to earth;
A slave was he of meek and lowly birth;
A bondsman dared not even raise his voice,
Nor o'er his young, his darling child rejoice.

But God his promises, has ever kept,
And the foul stigma from this land is swept—
At last the slavish chains forever broke,
And falls at last the bondman's galling yoke.

As they march on you hear their steady tread,
With ALLEN's banner waving overhead;
The cause of Christ to distant islands borne—
O, flourish till the resurrection morn!

HE HATH NEED OF REST!

Why stand aghast,
THIS weeping, wondering throng?
  The warrior hath his armor bright lain down,
And now in rapturous song His Master's praise he sings,
While angels sweep their harps of thousands' strings,
  The strains prolong:
      His fight is over!

He hath need of rest.
  His weary bleeding feet,
That trod the field with ever patient tread,
The dewy banks have pressed. They tread the streets
    of gold,
His eyes the Saviour's face and smile behold.
  Say not that he is dead, but
      He hath need of rest!

A goodly fight;
  A glorious victory won!
At Jesus' feet the trophies are laid down,
And on the warrior's brow is placed the crown,
  For which he bravely, boldly fought,
And heaven's glorious plaudits sought.
  Now, with the ransomed blest
      His soul finds rest!

Weep ye no more,
Nor stand with bated breath;
Christ will his promise to the faithful keep,
The mighty warrior is but fallen asleep.
He feels no more earth's care and toil and pain,
Our loss is but his everlasting gain.
Arrayed in white, in realms of perfect bliss,
    He finds a needed rest.

Eternal joys are his,
Who to the end proves true:
Ye fellow-warriors in the gospel field!
Fight on, nor dare the battle yield;
Press hard the conflict to the gate,
Walk in the narrow path and straight;
Your upward way from morn to even press,
At last ye too shall find
    Eternal rest!

REV. ANDREW BROWN, OVER THE HILL TO REST.

THE fight was at its hottest,
  The battle 'gainst the wrong;
The valiant in the contest,
Both vigorous and strong.
Engaged in deadly conflict,
A solid phalanx stood,
A breastworks made of soldiers,
Even soldiers unto God.

Amidst the clang of armor,
And crash of cannon's roar,
There came a sound which echoed,
And spread from shore to shore.
Andrew Brown has fallen,
No confiscate was he;
A captain bold and fearless—
No thought but victory.

He's just received promotion,
To the army in the sky;
He's reached a higher station,
We shall join him by and by.
Then, comrades, do not mourn him,
Drive sorrow from your breast,
Our loss is his eternal gain,
He's o'er the hill at rest.

BISHOP JAMES A. SHORTER.

———

Lines Suggested by the Death of our Beloved Bishop, JAMES A.
SHORTER, who Died, July 1, 1887.

———

IT came upon the noontide air,
  Like thunder-bolt from clearest skies;
Stout hearts were clad in sore despair,
  And floods of tears flowed from all eyes.
Across the States and o'er the plain,
  And to the distant Isles it sped;
From mountain height to sea's domain,
  Flashed the sad message, "SHORTER'S DEAD!"

From lip to lip the sad news ran,
  From every breast arose a sigh;
Awestricken stood the stoutest man,
  Till hope bade all look up on high.
God still is just, allwise is He—
  What He hath taken He can send;
Bow down in meek humility
  And own Him! Trust Him to the end!

Our SHORTER dies—do we say dead?
  Nay, only sleeps to wake again!
Though earth affords an humble bed,
  With Kings and Princes he shall reign!
He slept not at his duty's post,
  Who was a mighty army's head—
He led an ever conquering host—
  He sleeps—say not that he is dead!

Heaven stood in need of saint to fill
   Some holy office on that day;
And angels, at their sovereign's will,
   Quickly to earth they sped away.
They sought one pure and true and good;
   They found in SHORTER what they sought;
Pure in his life and love he stood,
   And to our sire this message brought:

Thy God to-day hath need of thee,
   They whispered gently in his ear;
He looked the shining ones to see,
   And smiled while they were hovering near.
His ever-ready sword in hand,
   Directed e'er towards evil's breast,
Now laid he down at God's command,
   And entered into *peaceful* rest.

The startled millions paused in pain,
   Tempted to ask the reason, why
Their noble captain should be slain ?
   Then out of heaven came this cry:
" White is the harvest on the plain,
   And ripe this shock of wheat has grown;
Ye angels reap this perfect grain,
   Which I, with mine own hand hath sown.

A MESSAGE TO A LOVED ONE DEAD.

I SEND a message, my worthy Chief,
  For I cannot come to thee now.
Though my heart is o'erwhelmed with its weight
    of grief,
    At God's stern decree I must bow.
They tell me that thou hast fallen asleep,
    That thou didst discharge thy whole duty;
They say it is folly to sit here and weep,
    For thy life was complete in its beauty.
And purity crowned thy declining years,
    And holiness circled thy head—
'Tis folly they say to sit down here in tears,
    And grieve o'er the tomb of the dead.

I hear the soft tones of Thy fatherly voice,
    Saying: "Cling to the cross, my dear child,"
If after life's labors your soul would rejoice,
    In the sunshine of God's presence mild.
No more shall Thy soft voice fall sweet on my ear,
    No more in this life shall we meet—
Till Christ in His heavenly Kingdom appear,
    And our warfare on earth is complete.

So I send thee this message to-night when I pray,
    I'll give it to the angels for thee—
They'll hasten to take it, they will not delay,
    To bear it to heaven for me.
I would not arouse thee, I would not awake,
    From this thy merited rest;
Sleep soundly thou loved one, thy comfort now take
    Upon thy Redeemer's breast!

BEREFT.

———

I FROM my window looked at early dawning,
The sweet breeze stirred and kissed my face;
O, glad is every heart, I thought on this fair morning,
Earth seemed so restful in the morn's embrace.

In grateful attitude I stood imploring,
Sufficient strength for daily care,
My heart was pained at sight of badge of mourning,
That from my neighbor's door, swayed on the air.

It told me the "unbidden guest" had entered,
And claimed the darling of that fold,
In whom their blasted hopes had once been centered,
Life evermore within *that* home was *drear* and *cold*.

I sought the mother in affliction's hour,
My solace offered in her sore distress;
I pointed to the Christ, the only power
To cheer the heart bereft and comfortless.

And in my heart's great deep I pitied her,
Who, though bereft could sympathetic be:
Our mutual tears were shed—I childless was—
And in her inmost soul SHE *pitied me!*

RESTING.

—

In Memoriam of Mrs. Bishop Turner.

—

WE mourn to-day o'er our sister dead,
  But sweet seemed the rest to the weary head;
The hands were calmly laid to rest,
O'er the pulseless bosom and painless breast.
The lips are silent and closely sealed,
The love of the Saviour, her smile revealed;
The weary feet that so often trod
Rough ways that led to the throne of God,
They tire no more, but forever are still;
They've reached the summit of Zion's hill!

Thrice had she come to the river before—
The boatman tarried to take her o'er,
But the voice of loved ones raised in prayer,
Prevailed with the Master her life to spare;
Then through life's day she gladly gleaned,
For the dear Saviour on whom she leaned—
A cup of cold water, or binding a wound,
Samaritan-like she was always found.

Her labors are ended, her trials are o'er,
Her soul has flown to the golden shore,
Where saints are rejoicing in white robes dressed,
And star-decked crowns on their brows are pressed.
Yes, she has passed on to the glory-land,
And bearing the sheaves she has gleaned in her hand;
The conflict is ended, her victory complete,
She casts her crown now at the Lord Christ's feet.

IN MEMORY OF JAMES M. RATHEL.

CAME a stranger late among us,
  With us came and cast his lot ;
In the Master's vineyard toiling,
  In God's service chose a spot.
Though upon his features ruddy
  There was yet the smile of youth,
In his manly bearing steady,
  Deep impressed the light of Truth.

He had come to lands far distant,
  And with strangers made his home,
But his feet from paths of duty
  Never once was known to roam.
Firm of purpose, pleasing manner,
  Touched with fire from above,
Holding up the blood-stained banner,
  Zealous, full of Christian love.

Like the Master daily went he
  Here and thither doing good
In the haunts of vice and mis'ry,
  On "the solid Rock" he stood.
Young, but in the battle leading
  Older souls who faint had grown ;
With the youthful daily pleading
  That the Saviour they should own.

Soon, alas, his work was ended,
  By the monster stricken down.
Yet on Christ his hopes depended,
  And by faith he saw his crown.

In his dying gained the victory
    O'er the grave, and hell, and death;
For his voice was raised in praises,
    Even with his latest breath.

Gazing on our fallen brother,
    Gazing not with tearless eyes,
Ah ! we thought of his fond mother,
    Could she in our midst arise
See how loving hands and tender,
    Wrought the wreaths of lilies fair,
Stranger hearts groaning with anguish,
    Stranger eyes wept many a tear.

Though her heart is sad, but sadder,
    For we know it might have been,
Had her boy in shame have fallen,
    In iniquity and sin.
But the congregation passing
    Slowly by look to gain,
For the last knew that before them
    Lay a Christian free from pain.

Pain of earth, and care and sorrow,
    From the tempter's snare set free,
Rest thou!   In the bright to-morrow
    We shall meet in heaven with thee!
Fare thee well and fare thee sweetly,
    With the saints in glad array,
Time moves on, bears us fleetly
    Towards the Resurrection Day!

THE NATIONAL CEMETERY, BEAUFORT, SOUTH CAROLINA.

I STAND to-day on this historic ground,
　　Where many thousand heroes now at rest,
Lay in this sea-girt nook, while not a sound
　　Of life or drum disturbs each pulseless breast.

But in the earth's embrace they calmly sleep,
　　While peace o'er trees and verdant shrubbery waves,
God's white-robed sentinels doth keep
　　Their nightly vigil o'er their grassy graves.

And here they lie as in their ranks they stood
　　Upon the field of carnage, where they fell;
With noble purpose linked in brotherhood,
　　They broke the bondsman's fetters born of hell.

I read the names engraven here on stone,
　　Yet some "unknown" appear who fought for right;
But on the records kept on high, not one
　　"Unknown" is found. They're known there in God's
　　　　sight.

" *Requiescat in pace*" until the bugle call,
　　Shall summon ye with us to meet our God,
" Who taketh note of every sparrow's fall,
　　And chasteneth whom He loveth with the rod."

SOLACE.

To Minister and Mrs. Lincoln, on the death of their son A. Lincoln.

AS o'er thy loved one now in grief ye bendeth,
　A Nation bows with thee, its sorrow lendeth,
That ye, grief-stricken should's not weep alone,
　Above the shrouded form of thy dear one.

But, as we shed with thee our silent tears,
　For him who bore himself beyond his years,
Hope bids us cease and banisheth our pain,
　And pleads your loss, his soul's eternal gain.

The reaper cuts the grain and lovely flowers,
　Transplants them in a fairer land than ours.
The path to heaven rendered thus more plain,
　Weep not, press on, ye all shall meet again.

He nobly lived nor feared the shad'wy vale,
　Defied the white horse with it's rider pale;
The grave no terror hath, and death no sting,
　For him who fully trusts in Christ the King.

AN EPITAPH.

WHEN I am gone,
  Above me raise no lofty stone
Perfect in human handicraft,
No upward pointing gleaming shaft.
Say this of me, and I be content,
That in the Master's work my life was spent;
Say not that I was either great or good,
But Mary-like, "She hath done what she
  could."

APPENDIX.

NEWBURYPORT, MASS. }
March 24, 1890. }

MY Dear Friend :

Our mutual friend, Mrs. HIGGINSON, has written me, enclosing a Poem, which gives me credit for much more than I deserve, but for which I thank thee. It is a pleasant gift to express, as thee can, thy thoughts in verse among thy friends and acquaintances In this way poetry is its own great reward—it blesses and is blest.

I am very glad to give the "token" asked for in thy little poem, by signing my name, with every good wish from thy aged friend.

John G. Whittier.

REPLY TO WHITTIER.

PHILADELPHIA, PA. }
April 2d, 1890. }

To my Esteemed and Honored Friend :

I now assume the pleasantest duty of my life, that of acknowledging the cordial receipt of your most inestimable favor of recent date.

Cognizant of the weight of years you bear, I will not burden you with a long letter, while my heart out of its fullness dictates to me faster than my fingers are able to trace; but my joy is *full*; my gratitude *unbounded*.

I should certainy have congratulated myself upon being so fortunate as to have obtained even your name from thine own hand, and a *letter*, such as thee wrote me, freighted with rich advice and kindly recognition is PRICELESS.

God Bless Thee, and may thy passage to the land of the blest be upon a calm sea with zephyrs laden with the perfume of thy noble life's deeds to waft thy spirit's bark onward, and over Jordan.

Gratefully Thine,

Josie D. Heard.

OFFICE OF THE CHRISTIAN RECORDER, }
Philadelphia April 2nd, 1890. }

To Mrs. Josie D. Heard :

DEAR MADAM—Learning that you are about to publish in book form the Poetic Writings which, from time to time, you have contributed to the *Christian Recorder* and other journals, and others which have not appeared in print I write to congratulate you, and to say that, as " Snow Bound," " Maud Muller," " Evangeline" and " Miles Standish," are now recited in the Public Schools; so, in the future may be, " To Whittier" and " Retrospect."

Already one of your Poems has been selected from the *Christian Recorder*, by an Afro-American youth to be read in a Pennsylvania School, whose teacher and a majority of whose pupils are white   I am

Very Respectfully Yours,

B. F. Lee.

2–Cromwell Houses,
London, April 15th, 1890.

Mrs. Josie D. Heard:

I thank you and answer you, that we appreciate most deeply the expression of your sympathy in our great affliction.

Very Truly Yours,

Robert T. Lincoln.

DOXOLOGY.

GREAT God accept our gratitude,
  For the great gifts on us bestowed—
For raiment, shelter and for food.

L. M.

Great God, our gratitude we bring,
  Accept our humble offering,
For all the gifts on us bestowed,
  Thy name be evermore adored.

POEMS

—BY—

ELOISE BIBB

1895
THE MONTHLY REVIEW PRESS,
5 PARK SQ., BOSTON, MASS.

CONTENTS.

To Mrs. S. F. Williams, President of the Phillis Wheatley Club of New Orleans, La.:

Dear Friend: — I affectionately dedicate to you, this my first volume of defective matter as a token of my strong regard and esteem for your estimable character.

Though all the world censure, I shall be content if I have but pleased you, and feel myself rewarded should I see the light of your approving smile.

Your humble admirer,
Eloise Bibb.

PREFACE.

I timidly present this little volume to the public with a full knowledge [of [its many faults. Indeed, I sometimes feel greatly frightened at my own temerity, and wonder how I would feel should an able critic deign to censure me as I deserve; but, if fortune should place my work in the hands of some clever judge, e'en though his criticism might seem harsh and unmerciful, I should feel that his judgments would benefit me in the future.

Never would I have allowed these imperfect productions to appear in print had I not been advised repeatedly by my many friends, especially one whose kind aid and disinterested friendship I shall never forget, to place this volume before the public.

I have implicitly obeyed them because I am aware that "intense timidity and subtle self-criticism" retard success equally as much as arrogance and conceit.   E. B.

IN MEMORIAM FREDERICK DOUGLASS.

O Death! why dost thou steal the great,
With grudging like to strongest hate,
And rob the world of giant minds,
For whom all nature mourns and pines.

So few have we upon the earth,
Whom God ennobled at their birth,
With genius stamped upon their souls,
That guides, directs, persuades, controls.

So few who scorn the joys of life,
And labor in contending strife,
With zeal increased and strength of ten,
To ameliorate the ills of men.

So few who keep a record clean,
Amid temptations strong and keen;
Who live laborious days and nights,
And shun the storms of passion's blights.

O, why cannot these linger here,
As lights upon this planet drear;
Forever in the public sight,
To lead us always to the right?

O Douglass! thou wert 'mong the few
Who struggles and temptations knew,
Yet bravely mounted towering heights,
Amazing both to blacks and whites.

The sons of Ham feel desolate
Without thee, O Douglass the Great;
A nation's tears fall now with mine,
While mourning at thy sacred shrine.

IN MEMORY OF ARTHUR CLEMENT WILLIAMS.

"Alas! that such a soul should taste of
    death,"
Such lofty genius fade for want of breath,
Such wit find refuge 'mong the mournful
    dead,—
    Such brains lie silent in that narrow bed.

O, let the Negro weep most bitter tears!
    Our brightest star from earth now disap-
      pears;
He would have stretched Ethiopia's hand
    to God
    Had Death not early placed him 'neath
    the sod.

Ne'er breathed a man who saw that classic
    brow,
    That did not then within himself allow
He saw a fixed desire to raise his race,
    Imprinted on that noble, comely face.

There is one thought that pains me much
    to-night,

Although of him I sing and sometimes
write,
I did not know this brave and gifted one,
This gallant youth,— this good, obedient
son.

Yet, ne'er-the-less, I sighed when others
sighed ;
I wept to think of fondest hopes denied,—
Of fleeting joys, of earthly woes and cares,
Of all that mother's tears and anxious
prayers.

That soul so loved by all now rests in peace,
He's happy there where cares and sorrows
cease ;
In that celestial home he dwells to-night,
That place of love, of joy, of dazzling light.

(Son of Mrs. S. F. Williams. Written for
the anniversary of his twenty-second birth-
day, August 23, 1891.)

EARLY SPRING.

The early spring's sweet blush,
Like a maiden's beauteous flush,
Mounts the cheek of earth and sky,
With radiance soft and shy.
She comes like a virgin queen,
From her couch of emerald green,
Enrobed in garments bright,
With sunny locks of light
And gladness in her smile,
Beguiling care the while,
With music from the thrush,
And the brook's low warbling rush.
She stoops and whispers low,
To the violets 'neath the snow,
On bended knee she peeps,
In the home where the clover sleeps ;
Her warm and fragrant breath
Has chased the gloom of death,
That shrouded tree and sky,
When winter's tears were nigh.
She dotes on the light and shade,
Her curls and mantle made.
O, ye who weep and sigh !
Bid tears a long good-bye ;

Be not now overcast
With scenes of the buried past ;
Forget the pangs of yore,
That made thy bosom sore ;
Know that the soul grows strong
In battles great and long.
Weep not, nor e'en be sad,
Rejoice, for the world is glad !

CLASS SONG OF '91.

We are sighing, for time is flying,
　　We are going from those so dear;
Friends are severed, though 'round us
　　　　gathered,
　　With a cheer to greet us here.
Hope is beck'ning, our fate we're reck'ning,
　　Life seems bright, all earth is light;
Stars are gleaming, beacons of meaning,
　　Lights of truth to human sight.

CHORUS.

Then, fare you well, fare you well,
　　Life for us has just begun;
Don't regret, ne'er forget
　　This dear class of ninety one.

　　Hours of pleasure, our mem'ries treasure,
　　Life's best moments for these we sigh;
Thoughts of gladness will scatter sadness,
　　When we're dreaming of days gone by.
We are sighing, for time is flying,
　　Soon we part from friends so dear;
Guiding teachers, God's favor'd creatures,
　　Ah! good-bye to all friends here.

　　(Sung to the air of "What Care I," by
Alice Hawthorne.")

ELIZA IN UNCLE TOM'S CABIN.

HER MARRIAGE.

I.

See! the moon is smiling
  Down her brightest beams,
And the leaflets sleeping,
  Whisper in their dreams;
Hear the merry music,
  And the darkies' lays,
Hear the happy voices
  Joining in the plays.

There in old Kentucky,
  On a summer's night,
Stands a quadroon maiden,
  Clothed in robes of white;
On her raven ringlets,
  Orange blossoms sleep,
O'er her slender figure,
  Bridal vestments sweep.

There we see her mistress,
  Smiling now with pride,
On her handsome fav'rite,
  Whom she sees a bride.
There is much rejoicing

O'er Eliza's match;
Misses Shelby fancies
George is a good "catch."

So the banjo's sounding,
And the darkies sing,
Hear them gayly dancing,
To the fiddle's ring.
But the dawn is breaking,
Guests must now disperse;
Quick the bow is silent,
Ere the sunlight bursts.

II.

The moon now shines upon a scene,
Much different from the one we left:
A mother gazes on her babe,
A mother feeling richly blest.

A smile of pride plays on her face,
A light of love shines in her eye.
She moves one black curl from its place,
And kisses it with many a sigh.
Ah! a mother's love is great,
E'en a slave could love and hate.
Swift the mother's blood ran cold,
When she knew her boy was sold.

III.

Haste thee, mother, pluck thy flower,
From the bed thou lov'st so well ;
Plant it in a soil congenial,—
Quick ! or they'll thy flower sell.
How that mother tore her tresses,
When she learned they sold her bud ;
Neither sigh nor tear escaped her,
Only her poor heart dropt blood.

" I will save thee, I'll rescue thee ! "
Cried the mother with new life,
" Though my life's blood perish for it,
You'll be free from all this strife."
Close she wrapped her life, her treasure,
Quick she steals out in the night,
All things dear she bids farewell to,
Then she disappears from sight.

IV.

" Farewell ! farewell ! " Eliza cried,
" Old home, I loved so well ;
Farewell ! dear trees and shady groves,
I'll miss your magic spell.
' Neath shrubs like these oft have I played,
These groves have sheltered me,

Just such a night my heart was won,
    Beneath that old beech tree."

With hurrying feet, she quickly sped
    Across the frosty ground ;
Her fears were roused with awful dread,
    At every quaking sound.
At length she neared the river's side,
    Her blood turned cold with fright ;
Those huge green blocks of floating ice
    Will land no boat to-night.

She heard a voice — the voice of Sam,
    And saw Haley, the man
Who bought her child, her all and all,
    She clasped her boy and ran.
The trader watched her disappear
    Far down the river's bank,
And when he saw her desperate leap,
    All hope within him sank.

She vaulted o'er the current swift,
    The ice now creaked beneath ;
She leaps, she slips, she stands again,
    Upon the river's reef.
Her shoes are are gone, her feet are cut,
    The water's dyed with blood,

With mad'ning shrieks she stumbled on,
  Forgetful of the flood.

She sees a man, as in a dream,
  Upon the other side ;
She hears a voice — her heart is still,
  " O, aid me, sir ! " she cried ;
" O, hide me quick, they've sold my boy,—
  This child I'd die to save."
" Go thar," he said, " to them kind folks,
  They'd save you from the grave."

V.

Eliza slept and dreamed of peace,
  Of lands where all is rest ;
Of bright, green shores where sorrows cease,
  Of homes which God had blest.

She dreamed her child was happy there,
  A free and merry boy ;
She felt that God had heard her prayer,
  And filled her life with joy.

She heard a step, she felt a tear
  Upon her forehead fall ;
She knew that he she loved was near,—
  Her husband and her all.

VI.

Farewell! farewell! our time is spent,
    We leave thee now in peace;
At last thou'rt free and highly blest,
    May heaven thy joys increase.

Thy dear ones all around thee now,
    Are bent in tearful prayer;
Their grateful words ascend to Him
    Who brought them safely there.

But we to-day lift up our hearts,
    And kneel in prayer with thee;
We bless the God who broke the chain,
    And set thy people free.

IMOGENE.

We had been school-mates,—she and I,—
How sad, those years have all rolled by.
I loved her with a school-boy's heart,
A love from which I'll never part.
Though vultures tore my heart in twain,
Still would it beat for her again.

With fancy's eyes I see again,
The old school-house within the glen.
I see the master, bell in hand,
The ranks in single file command.
I feel my heart within me bound,
I welcome so the gladsome sound.

But now I'm tired of ball and bat;
Beneath a large, old oak I sat,
And watched the girls intent at play
With hearts so light and spirits gay.
Oh, that life's morning could return !
For boyhood's days I'll ever yearn.

And as I sat beneath the tree,
I saw a maiden watching me,
But when I looked with smile benign,
She quickly turned her eyes from mine.
A maiden blush o'er-spread her face ;
She turned from me with nat'ral grace.

The maid was very fair to see,
And shy and prim as maid could be ;
My boyish heart began to beat,
I rose and begged she'd have my seat.
But high she held her shapely head,
" I care not for it, sir," she said.

Advances after that were vain,
She treated me with cold disdain.
And still I tried with strongest will,
But she remained persistent still.
Ah ! Imogene, had I but known,
We'd then had little need to mourn.

But Cupid's bow had touched my heart,
I struggled from that love to part.
A boy no more, a man to be
From that bright hour she gazed at me.
The hopes of youth had long been o'er,
I vowed I'd live, and love no more.

And gradually the years passed by :
My life was wrecked, I wished to die.
My mother, on her dying bed,
Implored an heiress I would wed.
My wife was very fair to see,
But not the one beloved by me.

II. [THE BALCONY SCENE].

The moon shone bright one cloudless night,
The earth was bathed in silver light.
I strolled along, quite tired of life,
I longed to rid myself of strife.
In vain I struggled to forget,
Oh, how I loathed the day we met.

I came upon a mansion bright,
From every window streamed the light;
Sweet strains of music reached my ear,
And peals of laughter loud and clear.
"Ah! this gay throng, I quickly see,
Would be no place for woeful me."

I hurried on. But hark! Just see,
Who is this walks yon balcony
All clothed in pure, seraphic white?—
I *know* that form, e'en though 'tis night.
I've heard that voice,—can it be true?
My Imogene, say—is it you?

Be still, she speaks; my God! 'tis she!
Oh, list! my darling speaks of me,—
Of me, whom I believed she loathed;
Oh, can it be her love was clothed
Within a garb of blackest hate?

But now the knowledge comes too late.

"O love, come back!" I hear her cry,
"My Waldershaw, for *thee* I sigh!
My heart was thine *long* years ago,
Didst thou not see? Didst thou not know?
Alas! I kept the secret well,—
This love will be my funeral knell."

She wrings her hands in silent woe;
O God! I watch her shadow go
From off the lonely balcony,
And leave me sighing mournfully.
A still, small voice I've learned to hate,
Within me whispered, "T'is—too late."

III.

These prison-walls are bleak and drear;
Who would have thought *I'd* enter here.
They say four men will die to-day;
My blood, also, will ebb away.
Ah, well! 'tis sweet to die for love,
That sacred essence from above.

That wretch which spoke my darling's name
With free license in homes of shame,
Deserved to die, just as he did.
I killed him,—though the law forbid;

The slaughter of man's fellow-man,
His blood o'er heath and flower ran.

I hear a step. Who may it be ?
Some friend who comes to pity me.
A comely youth, his face is hid,
His eyes are drooped beneath their lid.
The jailer locks and bars the door,
I see the light of day no more.

Who is this form that o'er me bends,
And rapture to my spirit lends ?
"What! Imogene, who brings *thee* here
To this bleak prison, dark and drear ?
Why weepest thou ? 'tis for the best,
I'll pass *from* woe *to realms* of rest."

Why does she hold her kerchief near
My nostrils ? Sure, she is sincere !
A stupor deadens limb and will,
My brain receives impressions still,—
But Oh, a deadness grips my heart ;
Can it be true from life I part ?

I see her change *her* garb for mine,
I watch her scrawl a single line,
I hear her cry, " Yes, love, I sigh
That I but once for thee can die ;

Far better had'st thou never seen
The proud, but faithful Imogene."

I hear her fall upon the ground.
The jailor enters at the sound,
And bears me from the darkened cell.
And Imogene,—how can I tell
The madness of that dreadful hour!
To save my love, I'd *not* the power.

I knew no more, my senses slept.
Of brain, of mind I was bereft.
When reason cleared the dark away,
I hastened where my darling lay.
With maddened speed I neared the spot,
But there my Imogene was not

Too late! My God! I see my love!
O angels from the choir above,
Oh, stay that hand that deals the blow!
Oh, raise that arm that trembles so!
My God! too late! the last I've seen
Of her I love, lost Imogene.

DESTINY.

In far-off England, years ago,
　There dwelt a wise old sage
Who, from the book of future years
　Could tare for you a page.
One day there came into his home
　A youth of noble birth,
Who asked that he'd unfold to him
　His mission on the earth.

"Lord Allsmere," spoke the rev'rend sage,
　"This day is born for you
A wife, in far-off Italy,
　For whom, one day, you'll sue.
Your bride is born of humble birth,
　No gold or lands has she;
But you will love her just the same,
　However poor she be."

" What!—I? How dare you say these things
　To me, Lord Allsmere's heir!
I take a beggar for my wife,
　With me my wealth to share?
Ha! Ha! a fool you think me then.
　I'll let my chances slip,
And leave the wealth of all the land
　To kiss a pauper's lip!"

You'll see, young man," the sage replied,
　" That all I've said is true.
In Venice, near the riverside

A bride is born for you.
You'll know her by a blood-red mark
    That stains her slender arm ;
Upon that mark a leaf is traced,
    Quite like a stately palm."

" I'll die before I'll bring such shame
    Upon my noble home ;
I'll seek this child, and murder her,
    And then o'er seas I'll roam.
'Tis well you've told me where she bides ;
    I'll leave England to-night.
Farewell, old man, you'll see that I
    Will make this thing allright.'

Ah. man ! thou egotist,—how vain
    To fight against thy fate ;
Know thou the laws of destiny
    Are powerful and great !
And its decrees obscured from thee
    Thou trav'lest in the night !
Bide thou with peace, thou'lt reach thy goal
    Without the aid of light.

II.

The night was dark, the air was cold,
    The city slept in peace ;
A whistle shrill rung on the breeze
    But soon was made to cease.
Two men, both clad in strange costumes
    Stole near the river's side ;

They launched a babe within a crib
    Upon the flowing tide.

"At last, 'tis o'er ; the babe will drown ;
    She'll be no bride of mine.
I'll show that old phlegmatic sage
    For her *I'll never* pine.
And now, away to Lady Clare,
    The woman of my heart !
Oh, for that hour when we'll be one,
    On earth, no more to part ! "

Lord Allsmere traveled all that night,
    And reached his lady's side,
And pledged again his vows of troth
    To his intended bride.
And he forgot the lonely babe
    He launched upon the deep,
But God, who guards the sparrows' nest,
    Watched o'er the babe in sleep.

And when the morning's roseate tint
    Was seen to light the sky,
A stray gondolier saw the crib,
    And greatly wondered why
An infant's wail was loudly heard
    Upon the water's breast.
He took the crib within his boat,
    And soothed the babe to rest.

He landed with his precious charge
    And placed her near the gates

Of old Count Dido's stately home,
  Of whom the world relates
Is seven times a millionaire,
  With neither kith nor kin.
And there the babe was reared, and grew
  A maiden free from sin.

III.

Oh, list ! to sounds that cheer the heart;
  Stay ! 'tis the clarion's peal;
The harp is mingled with the tones
  That make the senses reel.
And from the water's surface blue
  I hear the light guitar ;
Some knight of Venice sings of love
  That is his guiding star.

And why this song and merriment?
  Count Dido gives a ball,
And his adopted daughter stands
  Admired by one and all.
And oh, who would not love to gaze
  Into those liquid eyes !
To clasp that slender, rounded form
Would seem like paradise.

But Mariann knows nought of this,

She see *one* form, *one* face ;
She hears the music of one voice,
    She notes the air of grace
That marks her hero from the rest.
    Lord Allsmere owns her heart,
And she not his ?—Oh, dreadful thought
    That makes the tear-drops start.

But see ! he, too, has stood apart
    From that gay company,
And notes with eyes lit up with love,
    The charms that others see.
" Ye stars ! I've *never* loved before,"
    Lord Allsmere cries amazed.
" I thought I loved the Lady Clare,
But pshaw ! my brain was crazed.

" I've loved a score of times, and *more*,
    But 'twas not love like *this !*
My heart's on fire with doubt and fear,
    Yet 'tis a state of bliss.
Oh, love, that wrings the human heart
    Who has not felt its pain !
Who does not know its bitter sweets,
    That madden soul and brain !"

Lord Allsmere smiles·on Mariann,

And begs a moonlight walk.
Her gentle hand is on his arm,
　And soon engrossed in talk—
They near the famed Rialto's arch,
　He finds for her a seat,
And lays his sore and bleeding heart
　With fervor at her feet.

And oh! the joy that thrills *her* soul,
　To know she owns his heart.
Such heaven, ah, yes! 'tis paradise!
　Will bliss like this depart?
Two arms she lifts, such perfect limbs;
　Her hands are clasped in prayer.
But oh! what is that blood-red mark
　He sees imprinted there?

He grasps the slender wrist, and looks
　Upon the lovely arm;
And there a tiny leaf is traced
　Quite like a stately palm
"The babe I drowned!" Lord Allsmere
　　gasps.
　"Say! how can this be true?
Explain!—I'm dazed!—Long years ago
　I sought to murder you!

" Aha ! you've crossed my path again :
    The sage then spoke aright.
Plebian ! Ah, no ! you'll ne'er be mine,
    I'll slay you, *sure*, to-night !
And who is Destiny that dares
    Choose beggar for *my* bride ;
Ye powers above, I pluck this thorn
That lingers in my side ! "

" Oh, spare ! Oh, spare ! I thee implore,
    I'll hide myself away.
On thy dear face I'll never look,
    Nor see the light of day.
I love thee ! Ah, my heart is sore,
    Why dost thou hate me so ?
And what is this that thou dost speak ?
    Pray tell, I fain would know."

" Alas ! I cannot do the deed,
    My heart a traitor proves.
He slowly hides his sword from view,
    And from his hand removes
A brilliant ring with opals set,
    And lustrous stones that shine.
" See here ! this ring will now decide
    If you will e'er be mine.

" If e'en in days that are to come,
　　I see your treacherous face,
And on that hand I loathe and spurn,
　　This ring finds not its place,
I swear to you this night in truth—
　　I swear I'll have your *heart!*
And if, instead, you wear this ring,
　　We'll wed, no more to part."

He throws the ring far in the deep,
　　The water's sink it low.
He leaves her with an angry oath,
　　To bear this dreadful blow.
Weep not, O maid! dost thou not know
　　That thou art led by fate?
And it decreed e'er thou wast born
　　That *thou* shouldst be his mate?

IV.

Ten years have passed ; they've done their
　　work
　　On Allsmere's stony heart.
No longer proud, nor arrogant
　　He feels love's piercing dart.
He longs again to touch that hand,
　　To kiss that fevered cheek ;

Away ! he hastens to that land
   His destined bride to seek.

He sees her by the water's side,
   She kneels in tearful prayer.
"What does she lisp ? What are those
     words ?
   What is that sparkling there ?
My ring ! O Mariann, arise.
   My love ! forgive thou me !
My other soul ! I strove in vain
   To baffle destiny."

"Lord Allsmere !—See, I wear thy ring ? "
   The maid, uprising, cried.
" In yonder fish, the cook, yestern,
   By chance, the diamond spied.
And now, my love, no more this strife,
   My heart's on fire for thee.
Oh, thou canst never fathom, love;
   My heart's deep agony ! "

" Come, Mariann ! fate's chosen bride,
   Twin soul, I sought to slay.
Come to my heart, thou'lt never know
   A care I cannot lay.
Come, warm my life,—thou beacon-light,

Shine thou, this night, on me,
And I will bless forevermore
My planning Destiny.

GERARDA.

The day is o'er and twilight's shade,
Is darkening forest, glen and glade ;
It steals within the old church door,
And casts its shadows on the floor ;
It throws its gloom upon the bride,
And on her partner by her side :
But ah ! it has no power to screen
The loveliest form that e'er was seen.

Sweet tones as from the angels' lyre,
Came pealing from the ancient choir ;
They rouse the brain with magic power,
And fill with light that twilight hour.
Some artist's soul one easily sees,
Inspires the hands that touch the keys ;
A genius sits and wakes the soul,
With sounds that o'er the passions roll.

" Till death we part," repeats the bride,
She shuddered visibly and sighed ;
And as she leaves the altar rail,
She's startled, and her features pale,
For in the ancient choir above,
The man who sits and plays of love,
Has held her heart for many a year.
Alas ! her life is sad and drear.

He never dreamed he roused a thrill,
Within that heart that seemed so still;
He never knew the hours of pain,
That racked that tired and troubled brain.
He could not see that bleeding heart,
From which his face would not depart;
He never could have known her grief,
From which, alas! there's no relief.

At last she thought the fire had cooled,
And love's strong guardian she had ruled;
'Twas then she vowed to be the bride
Of him who stands at her side.
Ill-fated hour! she sees too late,
This man she cannot help but hate;
He, whom she promised to obey,
Until from earth she's called away.

This life is sometimes dark and drear,
No lights within the gloom appear.
Gerarda smiled and danced that night,
As though her life had been all bright;
And no one knew a battle waged,
Within that heart so closely caged.
The few who've never felt love's dart,
Know not the depth of woman's heart.

II.

Gerarda sat one summer day,
With easel, brush, and forms of clay,
Within her much-loved studio,
Where all that makes the senses glow·
Were placed with great artistic skill ;
Content, perhaps, she seems, and still,
She'd give this luxury and more,
To ease that heart so bruised and sore.

Her paintings hang upon the wall,
The power of genius stamps them all ;
On this material soil she breathes,
But in her spiritual world she leaves
Her mind, her thoughts, her soul, her brain,
And wakes from fancy's spell with pain.
And thus her pictures plainly show,
Not nature's self but ideal glow.

And now to-day o'er canvas bent,
She strives to place these visions sent
From that bright world she loves so well,
But fancy fails to cast her spell,
And sick at heart, Gerarda sighs,
And wonders why her muse denies
The inspiration given before,
When oft in heaven her soul would soar.

But now her ear has caugh a sound,
That causes heart and brain to bound,
With rapture wild, intense, sincere,
For, list ! those strains are coming near ;
She grasps the brush, her muse awoke,
Within those notes her genius spoke ;
An Angelo might e'en be proud,
Of forms that o'er her vision crowd.

What power is this that swells that touch,
And sends it throbbing with a rush,
That renders all its hearers dumb !
If he be man, whence did he come ?
Lo ! 'tis the same who played with power
The wedding march that twilight hour ;
The strains seem caught from souls above,
It is the very food of love.

And yet, he's neither old nor bent,
A comeliness to youth is lent ;
A radiant eye, a natural grace,
An eager, noble, passionate face,—
All these are his, with genius spark,
That guides him safely through the dark,
To hearts that throb and souls that feel,
At every grand and solemn peal.

Triumphant Wagner's soul he reads,
And then with Mozart gently pleads,
And begs the weary cease to mope,
But rise and live in dreams of hope.
The sounds have ceased,— how drear life
    seems !
He wakes from out his land of dreams,
And finds Gerarda rapt, amazed,
In speechless ecstacy she gazed.

" Neville ! thou king of heroes great,
A tale of love thou dost relate,
In tones that rend my heart in twain,
With intense agony and pain,
Forgive whate'er I say to-day,
Thy touch has ta'en my sense away :
O man that dreams, thou can'st not see,
That I, alas ! doth worship thee !

" Behold ! thou Orpheus, I kneel
And beg thee, if thou e'er canst feel,
Or sympathize with my unrest,
To thrust this dagger in my breast.
Shrink not ! I can no longer live
Content in agony to writhe ;
And death with thy hand given to me,
Will be one blissful ecstacy."

He starts, and lifts her from her knees,
Her features pale, and soon he sees
That tired heart so sick and sore
Can bear its grief and woe no more.
She swoons — her pulse has ceased to beat,
A holy calm, divine and sweet,
Has settled on the saintly face,
Lit up with beauty, youth and grace.

Neville amazed, in rapture stands,
Admiring hair, and face, and hands,
Forgetful then of hour and place,
He stoops to kiss the beauteous face,
And at the touch the fire of love,
So pure as to come from above,
Consumes his heart and racks his brain,
With longing fear and infinite pain.

The kiss, as with a magic spell,
Has roused Gerarda,— it seems to tell,
'Tis time to bid her conscience wake,
And off her soul this burden shake.
" Neville, forgive ' " with downcast eyes,
Gerarda sorrowfully cries ;
" I've told thee of my love and woe,—
The things I meant thou should'st not
      know."

"Gerarda thou hast woke the heart,
That ne'er before felt passion's smart ;
Oh ! is it true thou'rt lost to me,
My love, my heart knows none but thee !"
" Enough ! Neville, we must forget,
That in this hour our souls have met.
Farewell ! we ne'er must meet in life,
For I'm, alas ! a wedded wife."

III.

Why ring those bells ? what was that cry?
The night winds bear it as they sigh ;
What is this crushing, maddening scene ?
What do those flames of fire mean ?
They surge above Gerarda's home,
Through attic, cellar, halls, they roam,
Like some terrific ghost of night,
Who longs from earth to take his flight.

Gerarda stands amid the fire,
That leaps above with mad desire,
And rings her hands in silent grief,
She fears for her there's no relief.
But now she hears a joyous shout,
A breathless silence from without,
That tells her God has heard her prayer,
And sent a noble hero there.

And here he comes, this gallant knight,
Her heart rejoices at the sight,
For 'tis Neville, with aspect grave.
Who risked his life, his love to save.
And all have perished now but she,
Her husband and her family.
Mid tears and sobs she breathes a prayer,
For loved ones who are buried there.

Neville has brushed her tears away,
Together silently they pray
And bless the Lord with thankful prayer
For all his watchfulness and care.
" Gerarda, love," he whispers now,
Implanting kisses on her brow,
" This earth will be a heaven to me,
For all my life, I'll share with thee."

THE VESTAL VIRGIN.

Virgin of the vestal flame,
    Numa's child so chaste and fair,
Ah! Floronia is thy name!
    Goddess of the raven hair;
Weepest thou o'er love denied?
Thou canst ne'er become a bride.

Thou hast sworn to tend the fires,
    While thy bosom pants with life,
That the vestal hall requires,
    Hence thou ne'er canst be a wife;
Germ of death, Floronia fair,
    Sleepest in thy heart,— beware!

Glorious night! the evening air
    Shakes the murmuring fountain's breast,
Moonbeams now their lustre share,
    Gives to earth an air of rest."
From the convent's garden bower,
Comes Floronia at midnight's hour,

Deep in thought, yet still she hears
Light steps rustling o'er the leaves;
'Tis a phantom here she fears,
To the garden bower she cleaves,
Fearful lest some wandering shade,
Her retreat a visit paid.

" Ay, no mortal dare come near,"
   Thinks Floronia with affright.
" Guarded all these gates are here,
   Yet the vision comes in sight,
Sacred are these cloistered walls,
   Vestal maids receive no calls.

" See ! the moon is shining now,
   On his face she throws her light,—
Ah ! methinks I know that brow,
   And that sparkling eye so bright,
Lucius ! my heart's desire,
Why for *me* thou dost inquire ?

" Lucius, dost thou not know
   All such meetings end in death,
Thou wilt bring us both to woe,
   Love, thy boldness steals my breath,
Pledged to feed the vestal flame,
Never can I bear thy name."

" Ah, Floronia ! could'st thou know,
   Mine's a flame *more* potent still,
Sick my heart with passion's glow,
   Mad my brain with thoughts that kill.
Rome, for wisdom thou'rt renowned,
' Tis a boasted, *hollow* sound.

"Lofty walls and guarded gates
  Thwart not love's most strong desire ;
Listen, while my tongue relates
  How I quenched love's burning fire :
Deepest abyss, love, for thee,
Would I plunge, *thy* face to see.

"Tarquin built in days of yore,
  Subterranean passage here,
Lovers, aye, like me, before,
  Trod this aqueduct so drear.
Love, I beg thee fly with me,
See, I give my life for thee."

"Lucius, behold the dawn,
  Go, I pray thee, leave me here,
Mark the first fresh breath of morn,
  Leave this cloister dark and drear,—
Lo ! ye gods — we are perceived,
Warnings, they, no doubt, received.

"Lucius, I beg thee, fly !
  Go, my heart, think not of me.
Love, I *cannot* see thee die,
  Look ! — they carry chains for thee ;
Hear the virgins' dismal cry,
  Darling, thou wilt *surely* die.

" See ! the pontiff cometh near,
   Fly, my own, thou canst be free !
Seek thy unknown passage drear,—
   Lucius, think not of me !
Vain ! the lictors bind him fast,
They have stilled his voice at last.

" With those rods they're scourging him,
   Vesta ! save my early love !
Oh ! they tear him limb from limb ;
   Help him, gods, who reign above ;
Mark ! his large and bright blue eyes
Seek *my* face before he dies.

" Lucius, lost love, farewell !
   I will meet thee soon again ;
Short indeed was love's sweet spell,
   Full of misery, dread and pain ;
Ah ! they bind me now in chains,
   Soon released I'll be from pains."

II.

" Drear this dungeon, cold and dark,
   Showers of stones are on my tomb ;
They have left a single spark,
   In this bleak and silent room.

Slowly must I perish here,
   In this gloomy dungeon drear.

" Not a dagger have I,— none,
   O, to end this torturing pain ;
Poison, weapons — no, not one,—
   Wild my thoughts and mad my brain.
Lucius, call me, love, to thee,
   Set this tortured spirit free.

" Rome, thou tyrant,— barbarous land,
   Jupiter dost frown on thee ;
May Olympu's angry hand
   Set these tortured vestals free !
Dark my soul with dread and fear,
   Darling Lucius, enter here.

" Death ! — dost thou — encompass me ?
   Is it — thee — that grips — my heart ?
Come,— thou friend, I — welcome thee.
   True, — with torture,— now, I part ?
Lucius,— for *thee,* — I cry,
   Gods ! — at last — at last — I die."

CHARMION'S LAMENT.

Oh, for a drink, to-night,
Mixed by some god of might,
A draught of strange device,
Though of exorbitant price,
To give this tortured soul
The calmness of control!

Oh, for a cup of balm
From a kind and heavenly palm,
To soothe the aching pain
That racks this tired brain
With never-ending thought
Of the battle that *must* be fought!

Oh, for a potion strong
To keep the soul from wrong;
To give me strongest will
These waves of pain to still;
To ease this heaving breast,
So wild with deep unrest!

A balm I ask? For shame!
How dare I breathe the name!
What balm is there for care,
Except one heartfelt prayer
To Osiris full of love,

Who weeps for me above?

Away with sighs of pain!
Away with tears like rain,
That blind this tired eye
And cause the heart to sigh.
This truth I've found, I bless,
There *is* no happiness.

Ah! poets sing of love,
Fashioned by Powers above.
'Tis naught but fancy wrought,
A flimsy, graceful thought
As fatally false as vain,
Trust not the tale again.

They paint two hearts as one,
Who know no other sun
But the light from violet eyes
In their connubial skies
Of a love that ends with breath,
True ever until death.

Years have I watched this thing
Of which these wise bards sing;
Through Winter's frost and snow,
I've seen a spectre go,
Resembling Venus fair,
Which they do paint with care.

And when the flowers of spring,
To earth their fragrance bring,
This phantom, still, I chase,
I run with her a race,
And seek to grasp the hand
Which say they, hearts command.

And when the autumn came,
I watched her just the same ;
In rosy, fragrant June,
When time had reached her noon,
Forsooth, I saw her there,
Just as she fled in air.

She is a siren bright,
That oft your hearts delight ;
Garbed in a mantle black,
She heart and soul doth rack.
Not constant, nor yet true,
A bitter foe to you.

Enough, ye bards, of love
Fashioned by hands above,
That live, ye sing, alway,
And grow more bright each day.
Go to ! and tune thy Muse,
To sing us truthful news.

Nor tell me, ye, of joy,
Do not my soul annoy
With hopes that never bloom!
Better ye bought my tomb,
And laid me down to rest,
Than tire this weary breast!

I'll harden brain and heart.
Thy oft-sung Cupid's dart
Will never pierce my soul
Through the armor of control.
Away with pain and strife,
I'll live a restful life.

I long not now for balm.
This reckless soul to calm!
Keep thou, ye gods, your drink,
I fear not now to think.
The violent storm has past,
And I breathe peace at last.
(Suggested after reading Haggard's " Cleo-
patra.")

THE HERMIT.

The hermit sat within his cave,
　　A prey to anxious care ;
Distress sat gravely on his brow,
　　And suffering slumbered there.
His form is worn with constant fasts,
　　His eyes are dimmed from tears,
Within this gloomy wilderness,
　　He's spent full twenty years.

Yet 'neath the lofty, classic brow,
　　The window of his soul
O'erlooks a face where beauty dwells,
　　And strong emotions roll.
To-night, the tempter's crafty arts,
　　Repeated oft before,
Has stirred ambition's smoldering fires,
　　And roused the hopes of yore.

" Alone, alone ; " he sadly sighs,
　　No human voice I hear ;
For twenty years no son of Eve
　　Has passed this prison, drear.
No gentle hand has grasped my palm,
　　And with its feeling touch,
Taught me to value sympathy,
　　My fate has ne'er been such.

" And yet, my vision can recall,
　A bright but buried past;
The casket of those happy days,
　Too bright by far to last,
Is strewn with hope's dead blossom leaves,
　That withered, ay, too fast,
Ere fragrance lent her added charm,
　They perished in the blast.

" Within those crumbled halls of time,
　With fancy's kindly eyes,
I see a form flit to and fro,
　With beauty's soft surprise.
Her smile is like the April sun
　That gladdens leaf and flower;
Her tear of tender sympathy
　Is like to April's shower.

" A hermit, near to nature's heart,
　For twenty years I've lived;
And dark temptations cloud my life,
　In agony I've writhed.
But now, no more I'll linger here,
　I'll let the die be cast,
I'll live once more those days of yore,
　And breathe again that past."

II.

The sun has sunk behind the hills,
   The day has gone to rest,
A sweet repose has settled now
   On nature's placid breast.
A palace 'mong the Syrian plains,
   Is all ablaze with light ;
The king of Ansarey's divan,
   With splendor shines to-night.

Before his august presence now,
   There bows a stately knight,
The hermit of the wilderness
   Is welcomed to his sight.
His form is wasted now no more,
   And lustrous is his eye,
A strong conceit replaced the look
   That once was calm and shy.

" Thy majesty will hear me now ? "
   He asks with rising fear,
" I've loved the princess Fakredeen,
   This many, many a year.
Full twenty years ago, O king,
   Her shadow then was I,
And if you say me nay, to-day,
   O Sovereign, I will die ! "

"Most noble Englishman, Sir Luke,
   I've ne'er disclosed to thee;
A sacred Pantheon I hold,
   That is beloved by me;
Within its walls, the god of light,
   To Syria's heart most dear,
For centuries revealed to us
   Our future dangers here.

"Come thou, and Fakredeen, my love,
   We'll to the fane repair,
An answer to thy lover's quest,
   We will elicit there.
And if the gods approve the match,
   My blessing follows thee,
If not, then thou, O noble knight,
   I must refuse to see."

He rose; and straightway followed him,
   The princess Fakredeen,
The hermit of the wilderness,
   And subjects clothed in green,
Who carried with them garlands fair,
   They lifted to the sky.
As solemnly they chanted low,
   A hymn to Gods on high.

And silently, through portico,
   They neared the sacred fane,
Where sculptured forms of ideal grace,
   Serene and calm remain.
This noble hierarchy fair,
   The god, the nymph, the faun,
New beauties rise and greet the view,
   As does the sky at dawn.

They paused before a statue made
   Of ivory and gold,
The color pure and polished high,
   Displaced a matchless mold.
"The god of Ansarey, O knight,"
   The sovereign whispered now,
" My father's god, look thou on him,
   Thy knee before him bow."

" Before this figure, then, O king,"
   The hermit calmly said,
" Libations flowed from golden cups,
   And scores of steers were bled.
O god of light, if power thou hast,
   Give Fakredeen to me,
And with my pen I will proclaim
   Thy glorious deity."

"*I* must the god invoke, Sir Luke,—
　O god of Ansarey,
Shall Fakredeen be given away?
　Give heed, O god, I pray.
This knight from northern shores came he,
　My daughter fair to woo,
He is a Christian, sacred god,
　Will he always prove true?"

"Hold thou! O Syrian ruler, brave,"
　The god was heard to say,
"Unless he *vows* to worship *me*,
　Thou sure must say him, nay.
The God to whom he knelt in prayer,
　Who died at Calvary,
He must denounce, and live to prove
　A dangerous enemy."

"Oh, heaven forbid!" the hermit cries
　With heartfelt agony.
"An enemy to God, the Son?—
　Oh, that can never be.
My God! I *have* abandoned thee,
　Alas! 'tis now too late
To ask forgiveness, yet I know,
Thee, I can never hate."

"O Luke, my own, remember thou,"
　　The princess whispered low,
Those years of dark estrangement, love,
　　And all my bitter woe.
Admirers came, and suitors yearned,
　　My heart for *thee* did pine,
O Luke, forsake thy foolish creed,
　　And let *my* god be thine.

" Ah, Fakredeen ! my promised bride,"
　　The hermit then replied,
" For twenty years a moment's sight
　　Of thee I was denied.
O sovereign, king of Ansarey,
　　Say to the god of light,
That I *denounce* the Christian's God,
　　And bow to *him* to-night ! "

" Hold thou ! O Syrian Ruler brave,"
　　The god began anew,
The man who to his *god* is false,
　　To thee can ne'er be true.
Give not the princess, Fakredeen
　　To traitor false and vain,
Lest he to thee, as to his God,
　　Bring agony and pain."

" Almighty Father, wise and great,"
   With sobs the hermit cried,
" I see *Thy* hand beneath this cloud,
   That deadens all my pride.
That faithful heart, so brave and true,
   Was never meant for me ;
Farewell, my love, I go to die
   A hermit cheerfully."

A TALE OF ITALY.

'Twas eve in sunny Italy;
The world was bright as earth can be,
In that delightful month of June,
    When sun, and birds, and leaves, and
        flowers,
And e'en the queen of night,—the moon,
    Make earth one of fair Eden's bowers.
The wind was singing to the sea,
A soft and plaintive symphony.

The shadows of this placid eve,
To Count Villani's loggia cleave,
Where guests of wealth and noble birth
    Await,—with eyes more eager growing,
As darkness hides the views of earth,
    And stars begin their silver showing,
The entrance of the lovely bride,
Ninna Maso,—Villani's pride.

An hour or more they've waited now,
Anxiety is on each brow.
A sudden fear of coming woe
    Like weights upon their hearts are falling.
They'd give a goodly price to know
    What unforeseen event is calling

The bride who weds Count Villani,
The richest man in Italy.

And now the gossip tongues begin
To tell, in spite of outside din,
How Count Villani old and gray,
    From poverty and want rescuing
The girl whom he will wed to-day.
    And then their fears again renewing,
Their talk is of a serious strain,
Some fear to longer there remain.

But hold! a shriek, a piercing cry,
A woman's scream is heard near by;
And guests involuntary start,
    And move to where the sound's proceed-
        ing,—
That sound that seems to rend the heart.
    They look and see the bride receding
From yonder spacious balcony,
And hear her wailing mournfully.

In trailing robes of pearly white,
With loosened curls—a sunny sight,
The graceful form in flowers arrayed,
    As if in maddest haste pursuing
Some fallen Peri; this lovely maid

Madly sped on, her speed renewing.
What is her fate—her history?
Who will explain this mystery?

II.

'Twas midnight over Italy,
Still was the wind, and calm the sea.
The ceiling of this glowing earth,
    Frescoed with stars of twinkling light,
Whose orbs were bright with quiet mirth,
    O'er-looked a sad and mournful sight—
A maid in bridal garments 'rayed,
Beside the sea quite wildly prayed.

It was Ninna, Villani's pride,
Who weary, weeps by the sea-side.
Before her eyes the buried past,
    Like spectres of the midnight hour,
O'er saddened heart its visions cast
    With all their former maddening power.
Her home in Florence far away,
Her fancy paints as bright as day.

She sees herself in girlish frocks,
With golden, silken, curling locks
That crown a head and forehead high,
    Above the brows of velvet touch,

That over-look a deep blue eye,
   Where quiet sadness lingers much.
Within an ante-chamber dear
She sits.   A harpsichord is near.

'Tis eve—this time of which she dreams,
The dying sun has sent his gleams
To play on Pallas sculptured there,
   To light the ancient liggio,
And kiss the maiden torso fair.
   And while she sees the sunset glow,
A passion seizes heart and brain,
And bids her strike a mournful strain.

She wakes the harpsichord to life,
She dreams of peace away from strife,
" Of sunny isles of Lake Cashmere,"
   Of the sacred grass near the Ganges' side,
Where the plane-trees lie reflected clear,
   " And the valley of gardens lie beside."
She starts, and quickly turns to find
A man with face both proud and kind.

" This is Signora Ninna fair ?
I've heard of thy rich gift so rare,"

The stranger said with courteous bow.

  "And know this era brings to light,
As critics artists will allow,

  A soul aflame with genius bright.
O maid, art thou content to die
Unknown, and in oblivion sigh?

"Great Orpheus awoke the trees,
But in thy hands thou hold'st the keys
That ope the hearts of *human*-kind.

  O maid, the *world* will bow to thee.
List thou to me and thou wilt find

  A mine more rich than India's sea!
My youth is gone, my hair is gray,
Yet *I* will see thy famous day.

"Signora, thou must fitted be
To join this pictured pageantry.
To glorious Rome thou must repair,

  Where lives the giant minds of art,
And study with the masters there.

  From Florence, then, thou wilt depart,
And leave behind thy poverty;
They'll soon forget thy history.

"And now I will disclose to thee,
What I would have thee know and see.

This old, impassioned, foolish heart
  Dost beat most tenderly for thee.
Signora, Cupid's thrilling dart
  Has pierced an old man fearfully!
Hear me, Ninna mia, I pray,
Send not a hungry heart away!

"I only ask, O maid, of thee,
That thou'll bestow thy hand on me,
When thou for years have studied there,
  (And I, thy every want supply)
Where master minds of art repair.
  Oh, thou wilt ne'er these hopes deny.
Reflect on thy celebrity,
For thou'll be Countess Villani!"

"Oh, tempt me not!" fair Ninna cried.
"You offer gold and fame beside.
I care not for your boasted wealth,
  I *hate* the thing you value much—
The coin's more dear to you than health,
  That thrill you with their every touch.
But fame! That I could *tell* to thee,
  How dear a thing is power to me!

"Alas! if I will make my mark,
It must be done without a heart,

For I must *sell* myself to thee.

    This is the payment thou dost ask;
No longer gay, no longer free,

    Thou would'st confine me to the task
Of wedding, and of pleasing *thee:*
For *this*—I'll reap celebrity.

" Look down Via de Bardi there,
See yonder youth with raven hair?
He has a soul akin to mine;

    A poet's lyre he tunes at will!
My heart is *his*, 'twill ne'er be *thine!*

    When he is near the tempest's still.
Shall I for fame's bright, glittering page
These passions trod that storm and rage?

" And yet 'tis sweet to think of power.
Will I e'er see that glorious hour
When counts and princes bend the knee,

    And queens of every land will smile
With pleasure at my symphony

    While I their leisure hours beguile?—
Go, tempter, go. Call thou again,
And I'll give thee thy answer, then."

This scene of fancy passes by,
And Ninna sees within her eye,

While she thus prays beside the sea,
  The hour when she has bade farewell
To him she loves most tenderly.
  Her agony, no tongue can tell,
Yet she has given up all for art,
And e'en has trampled on her heart.

She sees herself in glorious Rome.
Of intellect it is the home;
And after years of study there,
  She wakes to fame of which she dreamed,
Surrounded by her votaries fair.
  Life, others thought, an Eden seemed.
But no! a serpent day by day,
  Slowly ate her heart away.

And now Villani comes to claim
The girl who'll share his wealth and name.
To-day, she was to be his bride;
  And while her maids her form arrayed,
A serving-boy stole near her side,
  And in her hand a missive laid.
Amazed, the words therein she read,
And this is what the letter said:

" Among the sick and dead I lie,
A voice within has said *I'll* die;

Before another fading day,
　　This plague that sweeps o'er Italy,
Will long have made my body clay:
　　But while I go I think of thee.
Wilt thou not let my fainting eye
Rest on thy face before I die?"

Then wild her shrieks rung through the hall,
Arousing guests, spectators all.
And madly rushing through the streets,
　　She swiftly neared the water-side.
Escaping all the friends she meets,
　　Who know that she's Villani's bride.
She wrings her hands and sobs that he
She loves should die so mournfully.

Just now she thought she heard a groan,
A smothered sigh, and then a moan
Beneath those sheltering lime-trees there.
　　Softly she steals, and lists again;
She breathes to heaven another prayer,
　　And quickly, wildly rushing then
Beholds her lover, lonely dying,
Beside the lime-trees sadly lying.

"Nello mio!" she whispers now,
As with her tears she bathes his brow,

Too late I know the human heart
   Is master of the human will.
Ambition's all-consuming spark
   Will ne'er its tender passions kill.
O love! my art has slowly died
Since I refused to be thy bride.

"'Twas thou who woke my Muse at will,
'Twas thou who could the tempests still.
With thee I would have touched the skies.
   My pinions into fancy soar;
Inspired by those, thy love-lit eyes,
   Imaginations realms explore.
But no! my soul on flattery fed,
My genius fades, and now is dead."

"Weep not, Ninna mia," he cries.
He moans again, and sadly sighs.
'Twas destined that our paths should stray
   Dear heart, such are the things of life.
We'll meet within a brighter day,
   Where there is neither woe nor strife.
Farewell! my spirit wings its flight,
Borne up by thine orb's softest light."

"Nello! I cannot see thee go
From out this life of mine, no, no!

Death sure, will likewise come to me;
  This torture cannot longer last,
My spirit soon shall follow thee.
  The plague its fetters o er me cast.
I die: my soul is borne with thee,
To the boundless sphere of eternity."

CAPT. SMITH AND POCAHONTAS.

The night hung o'er Virginia's forest wild,
  Stately with beauty unsurpassed before
Shone the full moon serenely ; and the wind
As it roused slumb'ring leaflets from their
    dreams,
Wakens alike the violet wet with dew,
And fans the lily on the water's breast,
Bidding the nodding petals sleep no more.
The crackling branches told a fire was stirred ;
Its light was dim ; yet, round it sat huge forms,
Like lofty oaks that near the watchers stood
With giant strength, spectators dumb, yet
    wake
With tenderest sympathy. The Red man
    decked
With plumage gorgeous, and bracelet bright,
With cheek besmeared with paint, and visage
    wild,
In solemn conference debated now.
Murdering Captain Smith. The forest still,
With a thrill echoed angrily their loud and
    stormy words :
The croaking of the frog had the exactness
    of a dirge ;

And when clouds from the moon were swept,
A prisoner bound in chains, with wan and
    death-like face was seen to pray.

An Indian maid, with slender form in rustic
    beauty clad,

And crowned with a wealth of raven ringlets,
Heard him say in tongue familiar, these
    words of deep woe :

" Alone, alone, I die.
    No friend or much-loved face is here to-
      night,
    To chase these visions dark from out my
      sight,
That blind my quiv'ring eye.
    Alas ! could I but live another year,
Much of the things I dream would I know
    here.

" How shines the moon to-night?
Divinely ! with a grace I've seen before.
    Ay — sick indeed this heart, these temples
    sore,
That could forget thy light !
Thou'll be the torch to light my light my
    spirit, queen,

From this bleak world to visions now un-
    seen.
" And this is life! Ay, life!
    Anxiety, dull care, a restless pain,
    That rouses, thrills, and sickens soul and
      brain,
A never-ending strife
    'Twixt the spirit and the flesh for right,
    And thus we ripen in a world of night.

" But see! they hasten now,
    Their consultation o'er, I soon will die;
    On yonder block of stone my head will
      lie,
And crushed will be my brow.
    Farewell, dear home and loved ones far
      away;
    Farewell to her who taught me first to
      pray.

" They come,— Alas! so soon,
    To die, O God! among this dusky crew,
    Where there is neither friend nor kins-
      men true.
Shine on, O friendly moon!
    Thine is the only white face that dost see

This savage crowd that seek to murder
me.
" My head is on the stone,
The chief with huge club bends to strike
the blow ;
A moment longer and no more I'll know,
But list ! I hear a moan.
Who weeps for me and mourns that I
should die ?
Who wastes on Smith a tear, or e'en a
sigh ?
" What ! the blow does not descend !
Whose form is this that clingest to mine
own ?
What means these tears and that heart-
breaking groan ?
An angel heaven dost send
To plead my cause and save this worthless
life,
That seems to love adventure, gloom and
strife.
" O, Pocahontas, brave !
Thou beaut'ous queen ! thou givest thy
love to me,
As did Dian, unasked,— an offering free.

Cursed be the treach'rous knave,
    Who would forget his manhood and
        destroy
    Thy noble soul, or with thy affections toy.

" Long livest thou, sweet maid !
    My bosom glows with gratitude and love,
    That thou wast sent as from the choir
        above,
This reckless being to save.
    How sweet life seems when snatched from
        death and pain,
    O God of love ! 'tis true, I'm free again."

THE WANDERING JEW.

" Toil! toil! toil!"

What curse is this sent from the hand of
God,

That man must work till placed beneath the
sod,

And see no recompense in future years,

Save anxious thoughts and bitter, fruitless
tears ;

What fight is this from morn till close of day,

To keep starvation's meagre face away.

Unjust proceeding, man's the slave of
man,

And this, they say, is a divine command.

" A cobbler's son I saw when quite a boy,

The mean privations that the soul annoy ;

And childhood's days, the happiest time
of life,

Was blighted by this same, disgraceful
strife,

Just so it was with manhood's happy prime,

And so 'twill be until I've done with time ;

And toil, and toil, and toil, thus, thus, I
must,

Until this tired frame returns to dust."

The voice has ceased, the cobbler's hand is
    still,
The sight he sees has overpowered the will,
    And hushed the vain complaints that mar
        his life,
    And fill his brain with discord, woe and
        strife ;
He sees afar a crowd of human fiends.

No law nor order 'mongst the group remains ;
    They all seem mad with mutiny and rage,
    Like lions lately freed from cell or cage.

Within that crowd a tearful, blood-stained
    face,
Where torture's marks had blotted beauty's
    trace,
    Looks up with loving, patient, sorrowing
        eyes,
    And seems to find its comfort in the skies ;
A crown of thorns is on the lofty brow,
And from his wounds the blood is trickling
    now ;
    He bears a heavy cross upon his back,
    The prints of blood are borne along the
        track.

The King of heaven and earth with scourges
  rent,
Endures with patience, woes His Father
  sent,
  And sick with pain, insulted by their jeers,
  The cobbler's bench he sees, and quickly
    nears.
" O friend," he cries, and seeks the cobbler's
  chair,
" One moment let me rest and linger there ;
  'Twill ease my fainting frame from half
    its pain,
  Refuse me not, I will not long remain."
" Go on, go on," the cobbler cries with
  wrath,
" No friend has ever cheered *my* dreary
  path ;
  And I shall never help nor give relief
  To you, a hypocrite and groveling thief.
This world for me has been a dreary place,
I have no wish my steps here to retrace ;
  " Go on, go on, *I've* known no rest below,
  I'll give *you* none, so hasten now and go."

" And thou, too, friend," the Saviour sadly
  cries,

With mournful face and melancholy eyes,
" Shall now 'go on' until the end of time,
And rest at Gabriel's solemn trumpet's
    chime."

He moves away and bears his cross again,
And stifles now his moans and sighs of pain ;
    On Calvary's hill with eyes turned to the
    skies,
    The God of love for mankind slowly dies.

II.

" 'Go on, go on,' I hear those words again,
The Saviour spoke them,— Ah ! with in-
    finite pain ;
    A century has passed and more since then,
    And still I walk along the streets of men.

Through Europe, Asia, Africa, I roam,
But dare not linger long at any home ;
    I watch the years go by,— the old, and
    new,
    But I ne'er change, I'm still the Wander-
    ing Jew.

" O God, I beg you, take the sentence back,
Remorse, like adders, soul and brain doth
    rack ;

Forgive a culprit's bitter words to thee,
And set this lonely, wandering spirit free.
Have not these years of woe and dark de-
　　spair,
With none beside my agony to share,
　Atoned for that black sin of long ago?
　Cut short, I beg you, now this time of woe.

" 'Go on, go on' until the end of time,
And rest at Gabriel's solemn trumpet's
　　chime."
　That awful voice, those words it seems to
　　say,
　O King! 'tis true, no rest till judgment
　　day.
O God! turn back thy universe I pray,
And I'll erase my blackest crime away;
　Alas! those bitter words I spoke to you,
　Have sealed my fate, I'm still the Wan-
　　dering Jew.

JUDITH.

O, that the years had language ! time would
    tell,
Of one bright night the moon has loved so
    well,
    For oft in darkness when she hides her
      face,
    She'll to the stars with energy and grace
Relate in her soft tongue the scenes of yore,

Repeat her strange experience once more.
    The night upon which she dotes.— 'twas
      grand, sublime,
    More perfect sure than any other time,
She bathed unsparingly the hill, the brook,
Within its depths a glance of pride she took.

O Juda ! if thou wast endowed with power,
Thou would'st describe that grand and solemn
    hour.
    In yonder sacred oratory there,
    Thou dost behold a woman strangely fair,
With classic brow and jet-like dreamy eyes,
Whose liquid depth outrivalled Italy's skies ;
    And pencilled brows 'neath glossy, raven
    hair.

Adorned the lids with silken fringes fair.
Though haircloth clothed that form of match-
　　less grace,
It could not hide the beauty of that face.

With hands devoutly clasped she's heard to
　　say,
"O God! send Holofernes far away;
　Let not that tyrant's hand my people slay,
　O pity Juda, Lord, again I pray!
My people all in agony and fear,
Dost pray thine anger soon will disappear.
　With ashes on their heads they mourn and
　　weep,
　Too overcome with anguish e'en to sleep.
Forsake us not, O Lord, for woe is me,
Forget thy wrath, and set my people free."

And while she prayed a ray of heavenly
　　light,
Upon her soul was shed,— all things were
　　bright;
　And with a vision cleared by sacred love,
　She saw her mission handed from above,
And rising cast the haircloth far away,
And 'rayed her form in garments bright as
　　day.

To Holofernes' camp with serving maid,
A lengthened visit to that tyrant paid,
And charmed his sense with beauty's daz-
  zling power,
And waited patiently for victory's hour.

II.

O sound the trumpets; let the bells ring
  out,
Their cadence has a mournful sound
  throughout,
  To merry hearts a night of joy they tell,
  To one they ring a solemn funeral knell.
A banquet Holofernes gives to-night,
And honors Judith who has charmed his
  sight.
  But he and officers have drunk so free,
  They fail their imminent danger now to
  see ;
Upon their couches wrapt in soundest sleep,
Forgetful of the vigils they should keep.

But who is this so near the tyrant's tent,
With eyes uplifted prayerfully is bent?
  Then softly rising, near his couch she
  steals,

With one wild prayer again to heaven ap-
    peals ;
Then from its scabbard soon his sword she
    draws,
And lifts aloft — and then, one awful pause
  Before it falls. She quickly grasps the
    head,
  For Holofernes, Juda's foe, is dead.
Rejoice, Bethulia, God has pitied thee,
And noble Judith set thy people free.

O, hail to thee, thou joy of Israel!
Thy name o'er nations cast a wholesome
    spell,
  Long live thy valor 'mong the deeds of
    fame,
  And may oblivion never know thy name,
Thou art the glory of Jerusalem,
Of dauntless knights, thou art the queen of
    them,
  Posterity will ever reverence thee,
  Before thy shrine all Juda bends the knee.
Stay thy rejoicings yet a longer time,
And honor Judith with anthems divine.

BELSHAZZER'S FEAST.

The sun has sunk 'neath yonder distant hill,
A hush pervades the world and all is still;
  And twilight shadows lengthen into night,
  That screens earth's beauties from the
    eager sight.
The city seems to sleep, yet, many a scene
Of sin, of misery and sorrow keen
  This hour enacted 'neath the garb of
    night,
  Most terrifying to the human sight.

But hark! — these sounds — are they of
    revelry?
What means this grand and pompous page-
    antry,—
  These notes rung from the harp and tab-
    rets's soul,
  That wake the brain and o'er the senses
    roll.
All Babylon awakes to view the sight,
Of lords and princes 'rayed in garments
    white;
  And mark their march to yonder stately
    hall,

Where sits Belshazzar, king and lord of
   all.

And here on rich divan of sumptuous rate,
This king of Babylon in robes of state,
   Has deigned to feast with lords and ladies
     fair,
   Who bow before his august presence
     there.
More beauteous scene the eye will ne'er be-
   hold,
Than all those sculptured forms in matchless
   mould,
   That rise above those towering columns
     grand,
   And seem to form one powerful, heavenly
     band.

" Beneath the porphyry pillars that uphold
The arabesque — work of the roof of gold,
   A stately peristyle in grand array,
   With moresque work stands proud, as well
     it may,
For artists would their souls mortgage away,
But to behold this work of art one day ;
   And from this bower of Eden, rich per-
     fume,

Like Brahma's burning founts, the hall
illume.

Belshazzar speaks, " I issue this command,
That all the sacred vessels now on hand,
　Within the temple of Jerusalem,
　Be brought to me that I dispose of them,
And we will drink, my wives and princes all,
Make merry here within this stately hall.
　Long live the gods of gold, of brass and
　　wood,
　But cursed be the kingdom of the good."

Why does he cease ? and why this sudden
　hush,
A moment past there was an obvious rush ,
　The tabret and the harp are heard no
　　more,
　The jests and jokes of king and lords are
　　o'er,
Belshazzar's face is of an ashen hue,
His joints are loosed, and why — his con-
　science knew.
　The eyes of all within that lofty hall,
　Are turned upon a *hand* that's on the
　　wall.

It writes mysterious words that no one knew,
The king would give to know their purport
    true
  A scarlet robe, a chain of priceless gold,
  His *kingdom* e'en, their meaning to un-
    fold,
In vain he bade the wise men rise and speak,
'Twas folly sure their import now to seek ;
  The queen bethought of Hebrew Daniel's
    fame,
  And mentioned to the king the prophet's
    name.

And Daniel entering in the stately hall,
Soon reads the words inscribed upon the
    wall ;
  He gave a solemn warning to the king,
  And loud the echoes through the building
    ring ;
" ' Mene, Mene, Tekel, Upharsin.'— see,
I will, O king, these words explain to thee :
  Thou art found wanting for thou hast
    been weighed,
  Thy kingdom numbered, and a section
    made."

"Bring forth the scarlet robe," Belshazzar
    cried,
With death-like face that bore no marks of
    pride,
  "And on his neck put on this chain of
      gold,
  And make him ruler, who these things
      have told;"
And then the kingly head in dark despair,
Was bowed upon his breast as if in prayer;
  Too late, Belshazzar, time for thee is o'er,
  Thou wilt offend thy maker never more.

THE EXPULSION OF HAGAR.

The morn hath risen clear and bright,
The sun displays his glorious light;
   Through heaven's vault of azure dye,
Where peeps the glistening morning star,
   And smiles the moon's great silver eye,
Ord'ring the dozing stars afar,
    Give up their watch, withdraw from sight,
    For now 'tis morn, no longer night.

A century's frost upon his brow,
Old Abraham arises now,
   With hoary locks o'er shoulders bent,
And wasted form and withered cheek,
   And faded eye to which is lent
A lurking sadness; it seems to seek
    Poor Hagar there with Ishmael,
    Who must bid him a long farewell.

Hagar," he calls, "take thou the boy
And go, for thou wilt here destroy
   My household's peace. Go thou, I say,
Depart in yonder wilderness;
   Ne'er turn again thine eye this way,
God will thy son protect and bless.
    Fear not. And now, take Ishmael,
    I bid thee both a long farewell."

"O Abraham! what dost thou say? —
That I depart? I must away
   From out thy home, from out thy life!
What words are these? canst thou be mad,
   Or do I dream? What means this strife?
Thy love alone hast made me glad ;
    O Abraham! *thou* hast been the light,
    Within these years of woeful night.

" And now behold thee never more !
This woe has reached my bosom's core.
   O Abraham! I kneel to thee,
Look thou upon thy Hagar now,
   Thou art a paradise to me,
Let me but stay to smooth thy brow.
    Let me but linger near thy side,
    Thou ne'er before my wish denied.

" And mark thy son,— my Ishmael,
His beaut'ous face,— note thou it well ;
   In yonder wilderness, the sun
Will scorch that broad and noble brow,
   And dark the cheek it shines upon.
My Abraham, O hear me now !
    Oh ! I would live in thy fond sight,
    And dream in thine eye's softest light."

Low bowed the head on Abraham's breast,
And to his heart a hand he pressed,
   And breathed a long and deep-drawn sigh
At length he slowly raised his head,
   And brushed a tear-drop from his eye,
He gazed on Hagar, then he said,
     " Begone ! Though it should grieve my
      heart,
     The Lord hath said that we must part."

'" Take, thou, the water and the bread,
I *mean* the words that I have said.
   Go thou into Beer-sheba there,
The Lord wilt guide and guard thy boy ;
   Lift, thou, thy heart to God in prayer,
And cease my soul thus to annoy.
     Again, Hagar and Ishmael,
     I bid to thee, once more, farewell."

" Alas ! 'tis true, I see, I know,
Thou meanest what thou sayest, I go ;
   And Hagar ne'er shall smile again,
No rippling laughter leave her lips.
The saddest 'mongst the wives of men,
   Will e'er be she, who sorrow sips.
     My boy ! my own ! all, all is o'er,
     And we are outcasts ever more."

ODE TO THE SUN.

How many scenes, O sun,
Hast thou not shone upon !
How many tears, O light,
Have dropped before thy sight !
How many heart-felt sighs,
How many piercing cries,
How many deeds of woe,
Dost thy bright light not know !

How many broken hearts,
That are pierced by sorrow's darts ;
How many maddened brains,
That are wild with passion's rains ;
How many soul-sick lives,
Stabbed with despair's sharp knives,
Hast thou above the skies,
Not seen with thy radiant eyes !

Shine on, majestic one !
Shine on, O glorious sun !
And never fail to cheer
My life so dark and drear.
Whene'er thou shinest bright,
And show thy brilliant light,
The cares I know each day
Silently steal away.

CATHARINE OF ARRAGON.

So tired ! so weary—
  The race—has been long,
And the paths have been rugged,
  The winds have been strong,—
And the heart it has weakened,
  In tempests so strong.

Soul, thou art sick
  With the fever of strife,
Of delusions of hope
  That will poison a life,
  Of a world that is foul
  With the passions of life ;

Of a world that is false,
  Souls that are vain,
Of men with a conscience
  Who live to give pain,
Of words from the fair that hide
  Vials of pain.

Of minds that are blackened
  With crime and with sinning,
That seek to ensnare.
  I am tired of the spinning

Of these ;—yes, so terribly
   Tired of their spinning.

So tired ! so weary—
   Of men and of things,
Of the woes of a life-time,
   That time ever brings;
Of the cares and the sorrows
   That life ever brings !

(Lines written to my dear friend, Miss Leona Hanna, on the presentation of a Christmas card.)

Leona, dear, twelve months ago,
Your pensive soul I scarce did know;
A summer's touch we did require
To wake the strings of love's soft lyre.

Accept this trifle, dear, and know
My blessing glides where'er you go.
May joy with her delightful breeze
Fan all your life, prays Eloise.

TRIBUTE.

(To the sweet bard of The Woman's Club,
Miss Alice Ruth Moore.)

I peer adown a shining group,
　Where sages grace the throng,
And see the bard of Wheatley Club
　Proclaimed the Queen of Song.

I see her reach the portico,
　Where muses smiling now,
Adorn with the green laurel wreath,
　Her broad and thoughtful brow.

Fair Alice! shed thy radiance more,
　And charm us with thy verse;
So dulcet, so harmonious,
　So graceful, sweet, and terse.

LINES TO MRS. M. C. TURNER.

Some bright thoughts visit me to-night,
  Of a lady fair to see,
  ho hides a faithful heart from sight,
    In a form of symmetry.

'Tis strange that nature placed that soul
  In a woman's lowly breast,
With all its noble self-control,
    And its zeal that knows no rest!

Work on, my patriotic friend,
  With increasing energy,
And God his choicest blessings send,
    For thy kind humanity.

SONNET.

(To Dr. L. A. Martinet, editor of the New Orleans Crusader.)

O thou who never harbored fear,
Who ever scorned her visage drear,
Who loathes the *name* of cowardice,
Whose banner bears the brave device,
" For justice, I will give my life,
Though I should perish in the strife !"—
To thee, I sing my humble lay.
Posterity will see the day,
When thy exalted name shall stand
Immortalized by every land !
Be thou our beacon over-head,
Ay, lead us ; blindly we will tread.
Until our dark sky is serene,
May thy unfailing light be seen.

LINES TO THE HON. GEORGE L. KNOX.

(Editor of " The Freeman," Indianapolis, Indiana.)

Know ye the man whom God has blessed,
With gifts peculiar to the rest
Of men who crowd the walks of life,
And battle in the world of strife?
E'er heard his thundering eloquence,
Or marvelled at the common sense
And flowing diction from his pen,
That soothes the very souls of men?—
This man who shines 'mong sensless stocks,
Is the great and famous George L. Knox.

ANNE BOLEYN.

           Lost! lost! lost!

The famed and gracious Anne is no more,
Her sceptre broken, now her power is o'er,
Ye judges, who, to-day pronounced my doom
With solemn words that filled my soul with
    gloom.
And Henry, king with deeds so just and
    and canny,
Come thou, and tell me if this still be Anne.
This sunken cheek, this tearful eye, this
    frame
So withered in its woe, cans't be the same?
My maidens, who, with skillful touch and
    care,
Have looped with jewels these locks of
    silken hair,
And smiled with pleasure at my face so fair,
When through the mirror they saw it reflected
    there,
Say, tell me if a likeness can be seen
In this poor wasted frame, to England's
    queen.
Ah, Wolsey. Yes; thy fate was like to mine,
I, too, did rise, but now, my lot is thine.

At once arrayed in pomp, endowed with
   power,
Now, fickle fortune assigns to me the tower.
Will naught but blood e'er quench king
   Henry's thirst?
Naught but revenge with which his brain is
   curst?
Base villain! though thou decked in robes
   of state,
Thy heart is like to Lucifer's in hate!
Thou dwell'st beneath a canopy of light
With soul in lust enshrouded, black as night,

And yet this man, so base, so weak, so vain,
Great heaven! this poor heart could love
   again.
Could kneel with 'raptured words and tearful
   prayer;
Bid him clasp me to his heart, and linger
   there.
Yes, he was loving, kind, and good to me,
Six.years I knew naught but felicity,
And gratitude, like some emitted spark,
Awoke the fire within my woman's heart.

My babe, Elizabeth, he loved the child;

Oft have I seen his countenance grow mild
Whene'er in infant voice she lisped his
    name ;
In tones like an Æolian harp it came.
But why this change ! How turned his love
    to ire?
Whence comes this wrath like some outburst
    of fire ?
False ! false ! O God ! the light has dawned
    at last ;
I know now why his tenderness has passed !

Ah ! I can see why he thus thinks me vile,
He basks within another's 'witching smile ;
'Tis Jane Seymour, my fair and gifted maid
Has made upon his heart this sudden raid.
O Father ! and 'tis she will reign the queen,
When I on earth, no more will e'er be seen.
She'll wear this crown I prize more than my
    life,
She holds his heart, 'tis she he'll make his
    wife.

O heaven ! for an arm of Samson's strength,
That I might burst these doors of wondrous
    length,

And flee this tower; sweet freedom breathe
    again,—
Ah! I would seek this treasured one,—and
    then
This dagger thrust into her siren heart,
And see her writhe in pain from its keen
    smart.
Then could I smile, and know forevermore,
Her fascinations and her smiles were o'er!

Delusion vain! these thoughts but poison
    peace,
And rack the soul with storms that never
    cease.
Lost! lost! lost! I've played the game of
    chance, and lost.
And O ye destinies! what it has cost
To brain, and heart, and soul! and now I
    die,
Scorned, and derided, and loathed by every
    eye.
O thou, who lov'st the paths of fame and
    power,
Know thou the darkness of this dreadful
    hour

Will yet be thine ! Oh, quench this fearful
    thirst,
Else thy life, too, with madness will be curst.
Thou'lt live to know thy hopes and dreams
    åre o'er,
And thou wilt fall, as I, to rise no more.

AN OFFERING.

Lord, all I am and hope to be,
I humbly offer, King, to thee !
When clouds arise, thy guidance send,
Accept my life, and bless it, Friend.

O Father ! let me rest in thee,
Resigned to what *thou* will'st for me ;
Content, though all my fond hopes fade,
And visions bright in gloom are laid.

When I was but a tiny child,
Thou shielded me from tempests wild ;
And gave me strength to do the right
Within temptation's treacherous sight.

And now in girlhood's solemn time,
Oh, make my life one perfect rhyme,
Sung to the air of sweet content,
With blended sounds of a life well spent.

VIRGINIA DREAMS

MAGGIE POGUE JOHNSON

VIRGINIA DREAMS

Lyrics for the Idle Hour.
Tales of the Time
Told in Rhyme

MAGGIE POGUE JOHNSON

Dedicated
to
My Husband

PREFACE

At the solicitaion of a few friends, I have selected several of my poems, and if the perusal of them brings pleasure to you, dear reader, the object of this volume will have been accomplished.

M. P. J.

VIRGINIA DREAMS

A Dream

I had a dream one winter's night,
It filled my soul with pure delight ;
Ne'er ran my tho'ts in strains so sweet,
I'm filled with rapture to repeat.

Oh could I dream that dream again,
'Twould be a song, a sweet refrain ;
Oh could I wake to find it true,
'Twould then my happy tho'ts renew.

Dreams, sweet dreams of the past,
Which o'er our lives bright shadows cast ;
Yet, sometimes in their course they change,
And pleasure clouds they disarrange.

What disappointments we do meet,
In dreaming dreams, yea, dreams so sweet;
Joy and happiness flow in streams, —
We wake to find it but a dream.

What is this mysterious way
In which we think we spend a day,
Awakening ourselves amid delight
Finding out 'tis not day but night.

'Tis a fancy which o'er us does creep,
When in that state of rest called sleep,
The light of imagination which does beam
And form what we always term a dream.

A dream is a miniature life,
Often lived in a single night ;
When pleasant, this tho't oft does gleam,
Oh could we live just as we dream.

When Daddy Cums from Wuk

Cum here, Mandy, what's you chewin',
    Take dat bread right out yo' mouf,
Do you know what you'se doin'?
    You'se de worry ob dis hous'.

Put dat bread right on de shef dar,
    Case 'tis much as we kin do
To gib you bread at meal time
    Till hard times is fru.

En Ike, you shet dat safe do'!
    Take dat spoon right out dem beans!
'Member well, you git no mo'!
    Y'all de wo'st chaps eber seen!

Yo' daddy'd be distracted
    Ef he knowed jis how y'all eat,
Case it takes mos' all his earnings
    Jis to keep you brats in meat.

Now, 'member well, you ebery one,
    No br'ad between yo' meals you eat,
Beans nor 'taters, no not one!
    Cabbage or bacon meat.

En, la sakes! here cums little John,
    Mudder's baby boy,
Wid my ham bone under arm,
    Lickin' it wid joy.

Gib it to mudder, honey,
    Cum, let's wash yo' face;
Jane, you set de table,
    And fix t'ings all in place.

Yo' daddy'll soon be in de do',
    He'll be hungry, too,
Hurry, Jane, don't be so slow!
    Ike, min' dar what you do!

Chillun, wash yo' faces,
    Put on dem aprons new ;
Be kerful, now, don't tar dem,
    What eber else you do.

Gib me my linsey dress, dar,
    Does you heah, my lad?
Yo' mammy mus' be lookin' good
    When she meets yo' dad.

Jane, take de rabbit off de stove,
    De hominy en 'taters,
En git dat smalles' chiny dish,
    For de stewed tomaters.

Leabe dat gravy dish alone !
    Mincin' in it on a sly,
La sakes ! mussy me !
    Who eat dat punkin pie ?

You boys stop dat fightin'!
    Sich noise I neber heahd,
Put de stools up to de table,
    Not anodder word !

All de eatins minced in !
    Dat's de kind o' luck
I seems to hab wid you kids
    When daddy cums from wuk !

I Wish I Was a Grown Up Man

I wish I was a grown up man,
    And then I'd get a chance,
To wear those great high collars,
    Stiff shirts, and nice long pants.

I wish I was a grown up man,
    Not too big and fat,
But just the size to look nice
    In a beaver hat.

I'd wear the nicest vest and gloves,
    And patent leather shoes,
And all the girls would fall in love,
    And I'd flirt with whom I choose.

I wish I was a grown up man,
    I'd try the girls to please,
I'd wear a long jimswinger coat,
    Just below my knees.

I'd wear eye-glasses, too,
    And wouldn't I look good ?
I'd be the swellest dude
    In this neighborhood.

Some day I'll be a man,
    And have everything I say,
And give my heart to some nice girl,
    And then I'd go away.

The V. N. and C. I.

Near the City of Petersburg,
    As seen by the passers-by,
In the neighborhood of Ettricks,
    Stands the V. N. and C. I.

A building loved by many,
    Who've toiled within her walls,
And tried to respond with pleasure
    To every beck and call.

Her situation is beautiful,
    As loftily she stands
Facing the Appomattox,
    So picturesque and grand.

Then in the month of September,
    As the days glide swiftly by,
Students leave their various homes,
    For the V. N. and C. I.

And ere many hours have passed
    They're sheltered within her walls,
Their minds from pleasures cast,
    To answer to her calls.

And for days, weeks and months
    Earnestly they work,
On their different studies,
    Trying none to shirk.

After the wintry days have passed
    The birds sweetly warble and sing,
While students resume their daily tasks
    They're told of the coming Spring.

And then on the campus green,
    Of V. N. and C. I. may be seen,
Students who every day win fame,
    Playing the many outdoor games.

Girls with tennis employed,
    Always enjoy it much,
Boys with baseball o'erjoyed,
    As with bat they give it a touch.

After a few years shall have passed,
    And boys and girls have finished their task,
No more their faces will be seen,
    Or voices heard on the campus green.

In various sections their lots will be cast,
    Fond recollections they'll have of the past,
As days, months and years glide slowly by
    They'll ever remember V. N. and C. I.

Old Maid's Soliloquy

I'se been upon de karpet,
    Fo' lo, dese many days;
De men folks seem to sneer me,
    In der kin' ob way.

But I don't min' der foolin',
  Case I sho' is jis as fine
As any Kershaw pumpkin
  A hangin on de vine.

I looks at dem sometimes,
  But hol's my head up high,
Case I is fer above dem
  As de moon is in de sky.

Dey sho' do t'ink dey's so much,
  But I sho' is jis as fine
As eny sweet potato
  Dat's growd up from de vine.

Dey needn't t'ink I's liken dem,
  Case my match am hard to fin',
En I don't want de watermillion
  Dat's lef' upon de vine.

Case I ain't no spring chicken,
  Dis am solid talk,
En I don't want anything
  Dat's foun' upon de walk.

Case ef I'd wanted anything,
  I'd hitched up years ago,
En had my sher ob trouble.
  But my min' tol' me no.

I'd rader be a single maid,
  A wanderin' bout de town,
Wid skercely way to earn my bread,
  En face all made ob frowns,—

Den hitched up to some numbskull,
  Wid skercely sense to die,
En I know I cud'n kill him,
  Dar'd be no use to try.

So don't let ol' maids boder you,
  I'll fin' a match some day,
Or else I'll sho' 'main single,
  You hear me what I say!

I specs to hol' my head up high
En always feel as free
As any orange blossom
A hangin' on de tree.

Thoughts

Had I the wings of a bird,
I'd make it a constant duty
To fly far above the earth
And gaze on it's wondrous beauty.

Had I the mind of a poet,
I'd always try to write
Poems of thrilling beauty
To fill some mind with delight.

I'd love to stroll in distant lands,
Among the rocks and rills,
And see the works of Nature's hands
And gaze on the distant hills.

I'd love to listen to the birds
That sing their songs of praise
And make some poor souls happy
In their saddest days.

It would be to my delight
To stand at the river side
And gaze on the placid water
As it slowly and playfully glides.

I'd love to write of the beautiful,
I'd love to write of the brave,
And read the minds of others,
And note their winning ways.

I would not judge the beautiful
By the beauty of their faces,
By suppositions or the like,
Or their pretended graces.

It brings to my mind once again
    The maxim that I love,
And one of the sayings as of old,
    " Beauty is that beauty does."

Krismas Dinnah

We's invited down to brudder Browns,
    On a Krismas day,
To an ol' time Krismas dinnah,
    So de imbertation say.

De deacons en der wives was dar,
    De parson en his wife;
En all dem folks did sho' look good,
    You kin bet yo' life!

De wimmin folks was dressed to de'f,
    Wid ruffles en wid laces,
En har all hangin' down in curls,
    Wid powder on der faces.

Der dresses had sich great long trains,
    We stood back wid de res',
As dey marched into de 'ception hall,
    To keep from steppin on der dress.

En de men folks wasn't fer behin',
    I'se here to tell,
Dey was dressed, too, in der bes',
    Lookin' kin' o' swell.

Dey wo' dese long jimswinger coats,
    Wid big leg pantaloons,
High silk hats wid broad red bands,
    En 'rived dar prompt at noon.

Dey wo' dem low-cut vests,
    Wid great broad white necktie,
En each man wo' an eye glass,
    Stickin' on one eye.

Ol' man Edmond Jones was dar,
    Dressed jis like de res',
It w'ud hab tickled you so much,
    To hab seen him look his bes'.

Him en ol' man Slyback,
    Was an hour behin',
Dey was ol' an walked so slow,
    Dey c'ud'n come in time.

Still, when dinnah time did come,
    Dem two was in de line,
Marchin' to de chune ob music,
    Keepin' ol' folks time.

Den dey stood up at de table,
    Till de blessin' it was said,
At de tappin ob de bell,
    Dey all did bow der heads.

Parson Reuben Jones was called,
    To say de blessed wuds,
En as he 'gin to cle'r his throat,
    His inmos' soul was stirred:—

"Heabenly Fodder look down on us,
    En dis earfly blessin',
We thanks De fer dis possum roas',
    All brown wid ash-cake dressin,—

"We thanks De fer dis sausage,
    En squirrel cooked wid beans,
En all dis nice fried chicken,
    Dese onions en dese greens;—

"En as we goes to eat it,
    Wilt Dou be our frien',
To keep us all from dyin',
    We ax dis, en amen."

De wimmen folks was helped fus',
    To all de kins ob meat,
En den we men was helped,
    As we sot dar in our seats.

Den we 'menced to eatin',
    Dat was a stuffin' time,
Case no one said a wud
    To pass away de time, —

Jis' 'cept to ax fer eatin's,
    Den in a quiet way,
Dey w'ud cle'r der throats
    En hab a wud to say.

You talk about folks eatin'!
    But neber in my rouns'
Has I eber eat up so much grub
    As I did at brudder Browns.

De wimmen dey was near de stove,
    En I tho't dat dey wud melt,
But dey jis kept on a' eatin'
    'Till dey had to loose dey belts.

En when dem folks did git up,
    Dat table was cleaned up right,
Possum carcass, chicken bones,
    Was all dat's lef in sight.

The Negro Has a Chance

As my mind in fancy wanders,
    While we figure on Life's stage,
While in queries deep we ponder,
    O'er the past years ripe with age;
While sipping slowly from Life's cup,
    And in tho'ts deepest trance,
This question often rises up,
    " Has the Negro had a chance ? "

'Tis true, they lived one life,
    Thro'out the darkened age,
When 'mid events full of strife
    They wrote upon life's page;

In darkest hours of the night,
    Their soul would seem entranced,
Wondering if some time in life,
    The Negro'd have a chance.

But now those days have gone,
    And on Life's page are blank,
And sons of ages newly born,
    Are being placed in rank;
Just as they file in line,
    To make a slow advance,
They read in front this sign,
    "The Negro has a chance."

The doors are open wide,
    That He may enter in,
And time ripe to decide,
    Where in life he will begin;
And as he slowly turns Her page
    He gives a quickened glance,
And sees in every avenue and age,
    The Negro has a chance.

With outstretched arms the college stands,
    And with inviting voice,
She gives the Negro Her demands,
    To make befitting choice,
Of the station He would choose in life,
    To make himself advance;
Now we've cleared away the strife,
    And the Negro has a chance.

Our race needs fitted teachers,
    Their knowledge to impart,
And elevated preachers,
    With the work of God at heart;
Men whose noble work
    Will have power to enhance,
Men who dare not shirk,
    But bravely grasp the chance.

Then heed ye to this call,
    Which means for a race success,
And what e'er may befall,
    Bravely stand the test;
Let not fickle minds
    Check your brave advance,
When every event shows the signs,
    That the Negro has a chance!

The preacher needs your aid,
    To help save Negro souls,
For the price so dearly paid,
    That he may reach the goal;
He begs with earnest heart
    That you lend a helping hand,
That in this work you take a part,
    And heed the Lord's command.

The doctor gives a call
    That you come into his field,
And as the sick and wounded fall
    To their weakened voice you yield;
He sees your help he needs
    As o'er his field he gives a glance,
And your steps he'll not impede,
    But the Negro give a chance.

The lawyer opens up his book,
    The leaves all dim with age,
And as he gives a steady look,
    And turns from page to page,
He sees a page all blank,
    And calls the Negro in;
Says he, " you fall in rank,"
    In law you must begin.

The skilled mechanic works his way
    As he performs his part,
He toils away from day to day
    And well displays his art ;

He loves his work with all his soul,
    And in it he confides,
But soon before he's reached the goal,
    The Negro's at his side.

The merchant takes his stand,
    With ready merchandise,
He meets the world's demands,
    And each day sells and buys ;
But soon upon the scene
    The Negro makes his way
And in the merchant's scheme
    He, too, must have a play.

The carpenter now stands aside
    To give the right of way
As slowly in the Negro glides,
    Now he must have his day;
In carpentry he'll show his skill,
    We may see this at a glance,
His soul with ecstacy does fill,
    As he sees his future chance.

The tailor in his shop we find,
    And as he cuts and sews,
He has his work upon his mind,
    For the art in it he knows ;
The Negro, too, has learned this art,
    And so with weary brain
He toils away with earnest heart
    That a living he may gain.

So, all these stations must be filled
    As we journey on thro' life,
And we must struggle with a will
    And aim to banish strife ;
And when we've reached the topmost round
    We'll send up notes of praise
To him our happy tho'ts resound,
    To him these songs we'll raise.

And Negro, yea, of Africa's strand,
    Ye strong men make advance,
We do of you make this demand :
    With vigor grasp your chance !
Let not these happy moments pass,
    But make good of each one,
And when you've reached the realms at last,
    And work on earth is done,—

You'll soar 'mid scenes of beauty,
    You'll live in seas of love,
When you've done your duty
    To reach that land above ;
And, Negro, be not far behind,
    But on, yea, on, advance !
And when you've reached that dearer clime
    You'll show you've had a chance.

De Day Befo' Thanksgibin'

Thanksgibin' day am now at han'
    In my imagination,
I see de tuckies take a stan'
    Aroun' de ol' plantation.

En jis befo' dis great, great day,
    Dey form dey selves in line,
En in a sort o' serious way,
    While one am markin' time,—

Dey marches 'roun de big hous',
    De gobbler front ob line,
To sho' de folks dat dey aint skeered
    Ef 'tis Thanksgibin' time.

De lady tuckies follows on,
    En, my! dey puts on airs,
As ef dey neber min's dis worl'
    Wif all it's toils en cares.

18

Dey's fixin' now to sho' off,
    Case dis am de fus chance
Since dey's had much meat on der bones
    Dat dey cud hab a dance.

De gobbler gibes a gobble,
    Den all de tuckies prance,
I tell you way dey wobbles,
    Dey knows sumpin' 'bout a dance.

De folks all in de big hous'
    Am comin' to de do'
To see what de tuckies am about
    Dat's causin' sich a sho'.

De ol' gobbler waits
    Till dey git outside de do',
Now he's lafin to hisse'f,
    Case dey gwine to hab a sho'.

De ladies ob de hous'
    Am now out on de lawn,
De tuckies gwine to run dem,—
    Run dem sho's you born!

Quietly dey tries to strut
    'Roun de ladies ob de hous',
While dey stans dar a grinnin'
    To see what dey's about.

Soon de gobbler gibes a gobble,
    En at de ladies start,
Ol' Missus, how she wobbles,
    I hear de beatin' ob dey hearts.

Dey am makin' fer de hous',
    Miss Carrie front ob line,
De odder ladies follow,
    While de tuckies clos' behin',

Soon dey falls into de do'
    In a sort ob mos'ac style,
De gobbler heads de list,
    Dey a yellin' all de while.

Missus calls out, Dinnah!
    Come here; come here! quick!
And kill this turkey gobbler!
    Come and kill him quick!

En when I got dar, what a sight!
    De ladies in a pile,
De gobbler pickin' wif his might
    On Missus lubely chile.

I grab de gobbler by de nake,
    Pull him fru de hall,
Tol' him take de las' view
    Ob Missus lubely walls.

I took him to de wood pile,
    Whar lay de cuttin ax,
En calls out, come here! Ephraim chile!
    En gib dis boy a whack!

Tomorrow am thanksgibin' day,
    En sho' as I is able,
Dis tuckey in some stylish way,
    Will be on Missus' table.

Ephriam raises up de ax,
    En wif all his might
He gibes de fatal whack
    Dat takes de tuckies life.

En Missus says till yit,
    As long as she is libin',
She neber will forgit
    De day befo' Thanksgibin'.

The Story of Lovers Leap

[At Greenbrier White Sulphur Springs, West Virginia, one of the
famous resorts of the South, may be seen the historic Lovers Leap,
which gave the inspiration for this poem.]

To the state of West Virginia,
　　During the Summer days bright,
Countless numbers are wending their way
　　To the Old Greenbrier White.

A famous resort of the South,
　　Which for years has held her fame,
And dame and sage of every age,
　　Honor White Sulphur's name.

'Tis here many lovers meet,
　　And stroll on her carpet green,
As the eve grows old, tales of love unfold,
　　And many just sweet sixteen.

Happy moments they do spend,
　　Yea! moments of delight,
As hearts in union blend,
　　They praise Greenbrier White.

Now for the places of interest,
　　Of one I'll venture to speak,
Which seems by far most visited,
　　Long known as Lovers Leap.

Where two lovers, once upon a time,
　　Whose love was true and tried,
Both with determined minds,
　　Ne'er to be denied,—

Climbed to this very high precipice,
　　Looked o'er the rugged steep,
Decided within a few moments,
　　To make the fatal leap.

Said they, "together we'll end our lives,
　　Rather than to part,"
Within their minds they did contrive
　　To make the fatal start.

All was quiet and undisturbed,
　　The hour was growing late,
For awhile they uttered not a word
　　As they tho't to meet their fate.

Their's was a love so true, —
　　Not for a day, —
Love that ever seems anew,
　　That never dies away.

This love began in childhood days,
　　As days so glided by,
They felt that for each other
　　Gladly would they die.

Perhaps many minds have wondered,
　　Why on this eve so late,
This maid and lad with hearts so sad,
　　Decided to meet their fate.

But the parents of this couple brave,
　　Firmly did object,
And tho't that both the lad and maid,
　　Their wishes should respect.

For a while o'er this they did bother,
　　Why think of the trials of life,
Now comes the words of our Father,
　　"Forsake all and cleave to thy wife."

Did it not seem hard for them to live,
　　Alone thro' the trials of life,
Could he on account of others give,
　　The dear one he wished to call wife?

No, "But together we'll strive to live
　　Or together we'll strive to die,
'Twill be a pleasure our lives to give,
　　And so with our wishes comply."

So, 'twas fully decided,
　　And on one evening late,
To the Leap they slowly glided,
　　The two to meet their fate.

On ! on ! to the fatal spot,
    The couple made their way,
To bring to an end the plot,
    Before another day.

As they reached the craggy edge,
    The couple hand in hand,
Carried out their fatal pledge,
    Their own, their last demand.

Side by side the couple lay,
    Hearts that had beat as one,
Ceased upon that final day,
    Their toils on earth now done.

And e'er since that gloomy hour
    The story has not failed to keep,
It seems some magnetic power
    Holds sway o'er the famous Leap.

Ne'er shall the hist'ry be forgot
    By those who the story seek,
But ever famous will be the spot,
    Well-known as Lover's Leap.

Why Should the American Negro Be Proud ?

Why should the American negro be proud ?
This question was asked in tones clear and loud,
The Negro who once was in fetters a slave
Now passes in freedom from birth to his grave.

Why should the Negro with eagerness yearn
For wisdom which teaches men how to discern,
Why should they with faithful hearts plead
Or yearn for wisdom that they may succeed.

Does not the same God who rules on high
Instill in the hearts of all mankind to try,
Is not the same God the Negro protector,
Why says, "Of persons I'm no respecter."

Then, should persons in ignorance plead
To know why the Negro wants to succeed,
When Nature's law in common states—
That human beings have similar traits.

The Negro for wisdom puts in a petition,
    That intelligently he too may live ;
That he may gain such recognition
    That intelligence might give.

In ignorance they lived for years,
    When they had not the chance to learn;
That ignorance to them bro't bitter tears,
    And now for wisdom they yearn.

The best of this race make good their chance,
    This story, schools and colleges tell,
Each year may be seen their steady advance
    As their numbers in greatness swell.

Then should the American Negro be proud,
    When each day he makes an advance,
As gradually he's moved away the cloud
    Which for years denied him a chance.

Then, why not encourage him each day,
    When he tries to make most of his life,
And live in a friendly feeling way,
    Casting aside all malice and strife.

Would not life be a pleasure,
    If the races would manifest
Such interest in each other
    That none would advancement detest.

Would not our lives be glorious
    If friendship ruled the land,
Making our efforts victorious,
    Regardless of race or clan.

What will become of the Negro
    When friendship's ebb is low,
What will make him a hero
    In the midst of an embittered foe.

The Negro must learn, if he would improve,
	And remove the many defects
Which cause other races to term him rude,
	And for him to lose their respect.

Among the White race he has some friends
	Who urge him onward each day ;
Gladly a helping hand they lend
	As he onward works his way.

Yet in the distance not afar
	He sees a heavy cloud
Moving slowly o'er the land
	Where Negroes are justly proud.

Will the storm's effect prove serious ?
	To know we can only wait ;
For in ways almost mysterious
	Sometimes comes a nation's fate.

Then, Negro, Oh ! Negro, cease repining,
'Tis said each cloud has a silver lining;
Pray to the God who rules on high, —
He has the power to clear the sky.

It is He who rules the universe,
And guides it's affairs for better or worse;
All earthly affairs are in His hands,
The whole earth moves at His commands.

'Twas by His aid and thro' His power
	The Negro has made an advance ;
He aids them thro' their trying hours
	That they might have a chance.

Should not the American Negro be proud
	When he has been given a start,
And tho' he discerns some heavy clouds,
	He should toil with an earnest heart.

Yea ! toil with an earnest heart
	And deeds of evil shun,
'Tis said that we're remembered
	By all that we have done.

Then, Negro, toil on, act well your part;
    Bravely stand the test;
Do your duty, be earnest at heart;
    Believe what happens is best.

And when your task on earth is done,
    And time for reward is at hand,
When at last the victory's won,
    And you view yon happy land,—

In happiness, in boundless love,
You'll spend eternity in realms above;
After having stood the test,
You'll enjoy, above, the rest, sweet rest.

De Leap Yeah Party

Was you at de hall las' night,
    To de Leap Yeah Party?
I reckon dat I was,
    But didn't I eat hearty?

I wouldn't hab missed gwine dar,
    Fo' sumpin purty fine;
Dem folks was sholy lookin' good,
    En had one sumptious time.

En ebery which a way you went
    About de day befo',
Some one was standin' at yo' fence,
    Or knockin' at yo' do'.

Axin dese here questions:
    Is you gwine out to-night?
What color is you gwine to w'ar,
    Yaller, blue or white?

Is you gwine to twis' yo' hwar up high,
    Or let it cum down low?
Is you gwine to walk dar,
    How's you gwine to go?

En ob all de questions,
    I neber heahed befo',
As dey met me wif upon de street,
    En eben at my do'.

Till I jis took to thinkin'
    As I walked aroun'
Dat dis would be de grandes' t'ing,
    Dat eber cum to town.

Case ol' an young was fixin'
    En primpin' up to date,
Leaben all de wuk undone
    Fo' fear dat dey'd be late.

En when I got into dat hall,
    Goodness! what a sight,
De same as pictures on de wall
    De folks did look dat night.

Cud'n tell ol' folks from de young,
    Case all was lookin' gay,
Chattin' to der fellows
    In a stylish kin' o' way.

En you better had been kerful,
    Dar'd been one de bigges fights
Had you called eny body ol' folks
    On dat Leap Yeah Party night.

Eben to de ol' men,
    Who'd always had der canes,
To keep f'om fallin' in de streets,
    Or slippin' in de rain, —

Had flung dem all away dat night,
    En cum in struttin' too,
Wid long tail jimswingers on,
    En I said, Who but you?

It wud hab tickled you so much,
    'Til you on your knees wud fall,
Could you jis hab seed dem folks
    A settin' in dat hall.

Like sardines in a box,
    Dem folks was sholy packed,—
Hardly room to draw yo' breaf,
    'Lieve me, 'tis a fact!

De music it was playin', too,
    Like ragtime at a ball,
De folks could hardly hold dey feet,
    But de parson viewed dem all,—

En dey was skeered to move dem,
    Or make a silent tread,
So dey kept time wid de music
    By de bowin' ob de head.

When eatin' time did cum,
    Dey all was at de table,
Puttin' 'way de grub,
    As fas' as dey was able.

Gibin no tho't to dem aroun',
    En not a wud dey said,
Stuffin' dey mouths wid chicken,
    Tater salid, ham en bread.

De odder folks wid hungry looks,
    Sot waitin' fo' der turn,
Hoping dar'd be sumpin' lef,
    As dey gazed wid faces stern.

As dey finished ob der eatin',
    Dey moved up f'om der places,
En turnin' dey did meet,
    A number ob smilin' faces.

Now 'twas der turn to eat,
    Sich a scrumagin' dey had,
En dem dat failed to git seats,
    Did turn wid faces sad.

Dey soon got thro' der eatin',
    Case de hour was growin' ol',
Dey heahd de clock a strikin',
    En de mornin' hour it told.

Dey called out fo' der coats en hats,
     Wid faces gay en bright,
En eber dey'll remember,
     Dat Leap Yeah Party night.

What's Mo' Temptin' to de Palate?

What's mo' temptin' to de palate,
     When you's wuked so hard all day,
En cum in home at ebentime
     Widout a wud to say,—
En see a stewin' in de stove
     A possum crisp en brown,
Wid great big sweet potaters,
     A layin' all aroun'.

What's mo' temptin' to de palate,
     Den a chicken bilin' hot,
En plenty ob good dumplin's,
     A bubblin' in de pot;
To set right down to eat dem,
     En 'pease yo' hunger dar,
'Tis nuffin' mo' enjoyin',
     I sho'ly do declar.

What's mo' temptin' to de palate
     Den a dish ob good baked beans,
En what is still mo' temptin'
     Den a pot brimfull ob greens;
Jis biled down low wid bacon,
     Almos' 'til dey's fried,
En a plate ob good ol' co'n cakes
     A layin' on de side.

What's mo' temptin' to de palate
     Den on Thanksgibin' Day
To hab a good ol' tuckey
     Fixed some kin' o' way;

Wid cranber'y sauce en celery,
        All settin' on de side,
En eat jis 'til yo' appetite
        Is sho' full satisfied.

What's mo' temptin' to de palate,
        Den in de Summer time,
To bus' a watermillion
        Right from off de vine;
En set right down to eat it
        In de coolin breeze,
Wif nuffin' to moles' you,
        Settin' neaf de apple trees.

What's mo' temptin' to de palate,
        Den poke chops, also lam',
En what is still mo' temptin'
        Den good ol' col' biled ham;
Veal chops dey ain't bad,
        Put de mutton chops in line,
I tell you my ol' appetite,
        Fo' all dese t'ings do pine.

What' mo' temptin' to de palate,
        When you cum from wuk at night,
To set down to de fiah,
        A shinin' jis so bright,
De ol' 'oman walks in,—
        Wid supper brilin' hot,
En a good ol' cup ob coffee,
        Jis steamin' out de pot.

'Tis den I kin enjoy myse'f,
        En eat dar by de fiah,
Case puttin' way good eatin's
        Is sho'ly my desire;
Dar's nuffin dat's so temptin',
        Dat to me is a treat,
Den settin' at a table
        Wid plenty good to eat.

Dat Mule ob Brudder Wright's

Dar's plenty t'ings to write erbout,
    Bof in en out ob skool,
'Cept taken fo' a subject,
    En ol' en stubborn mule.

But de one I specs to write erbout,
    Ain't ob de stubborn kin';
A fus class critter out en out,
    Beats eny mule in line.

At eny kin' ob wuk he's good, —
    Kin put him to de plow,
Or take him out to haulin' wood,
    He'll wuk from hour to hour.

Hitch him wid anodder mule,
    Or let him pull alone,
Eny whar you put him
    Dis ol' mule is at home.

You see him to de buggy,
    In de mornin's cle'r en bright,
Put him to de cart,
    It is his heart's delight.

Eny whar you take him,
    He'll make hisse'f at home,
Eny whar you hitch him,
    He'll stan' en will not roam.

Will I tell you who he 'longs to?
    Sho, wid delight,
He is de splendid property
    Ob brudder Henry Wright.

Dar's odder mules in town,
    But none so gay en spry,
Hitch him to de sulky
    En he kin sholy fly.

Not one lazy bone
　　Do dis mule posess,
In any kin' ob wuk
　　He kin stan de tes'.

Dar's plenty mules in town,
　　But none so out ob sight,
As dis thoro' bred Kintucky
　　Ob brudder Henry Wright's.

Dar's none wid no sich name,
　　Dat's trabbled on his way,
No, none wid no sich fame
　　As you read ob dem each day.

Dar's odder mules in town,
　　But none kin take de flight,
Or make a steady roun'
　　Like dis ob Henry Wright's.

Ef you wants to see some pacin',
　　Jis call on dis ol' mule,
When it cums to out right racin'
　　You'd t'ink he'd been to skool.

Dar's plenty mules aroun',
　　But none no whar in sight,
Not eben in dis town,
　　Like dis ob Henry Wright's.

No odder mule in town
　　Does know de roads so well,
No matter whar you take him
　　Dis mule can always tell.

He likes to wuk in sunshine,
　　He likes to wuk in rain,
At night or eben day time,
　　He always seems de same.

He neber jumps out ob de road,
　　When de 'mobiles cum his way,
Eny whar he has a load
　　Dis mule aint 'fraid to stay.

Nuffin cud'n skeer him,
  At night or eny time,
A match fo' dis ol' mule
  Wud be hard to find.

Dar's odder mules in town,
  But none no whar in sight,
Dat sho cou'd win de crown
  Like dis ob Henry Wright's.

Sometimes

Sometimes the days seem dark and dreary,
  We wonder what is life;
Sometimes of work we soon grow weary,
  All pleasures seem but strife.

Sometimes of aiming we grow tired,
  And finally give up all,
Leaving the mind once inspired,
  Heedless to a call.

Sometimes we give no thought to those
  Who in some way we might aid;
Sometimes others' pains and woes
  Are at our mercies laid.

Sometimes if we'd stop to think
  And count the good deeds we do
To help those on Poverty's brink
  We'd find them to be few.

Sometimes a good act we might render
  By saying some kind words,
To those whose hearts so tender
  By kindness has ne'er been stirred.

Sometimes 'twould help us to resolve
  That each day while we live,
Some difficult problem we will solve,
  Or aid to others give.

And thus instead of wondering,
  And making all efforts strife—
Instead of always pondering,
  To find out what is life,—

By our actions, by the deeds we do,
  Each day while we live,
Let them be many, or let them be few,
  We make life what it is.

To See Ol' Booker T.

Way down Souf whar de lillies grow,
  Is the lan' I wants to see,
En to dat lan' I specs to go,
  Jis to see ol' Booker T.

I specs to take my faithful mule
  En hitch him to de cart,
En fo' dat famous cullered skool
  I's gwine to make a start.

I'll take a box and pack my lunch
  En start wid my ol' mule,
Case I know 'twill be a long time
  Fo' I reach dat Cullered Skool.

I wont get tired on de way,
  But sing en feel so free,
Jis longin' fo' de day
  To see ol' Booker T.

I hopes dat my ol' mule
  Wont gib out on de way,
Befor' I reach dat skool,
  Case I tell you dat wont pay.

Case dis feeble ol' man
  Ain't no lad, you see,
But befo' I leabes dis lan'
  I mus' see Booker T.

So I pray de Lawd to keep
    Bof me en my ol' mule,
En spar us till we git
    To dat Cullered Skool.

En gib our eyes de light,
    Dat we can cle'rly see,
Dat Alabama lan' so bright,
    En dear ol' Booker T.

I wonder ef he'll be at home,
    Case I heahed he'd been to sea,
En all de fer off lan's did roam,
    Dis same Booker T.

Dat eben kings en queens so great
    Did strive to shake his han'
En welcome Booker T.
    To der native land.

Now, you know he mus' be great ;
    Well, I's gwine dar to see,
En ef I git dar soon or late,
    I'll ax fo' Booker T.

Dey say dat is de bigges' skool
    De same as eny town,
En neber was so many chaps
    Eber seen aroun'.

Day teaches you all kin's ob wuk
    En how to write en read,
En figger in de 'rithmetic,
    En ebery t'ing you needs.

Dey teaches you to plant de co'n,
    En eben how to plow ;
I tell you, man, as sho's you born,
    I'm on my way dar now.
En when I near dat skool,
    En all dem chaps I see,
Dey better had keep cool,
    En not make fun at me.

I sho' will bus' der heads,
    Case my only plea
Is dat fo' I's dead
    I mus' see Booker T.

Right in his office I will go,
    En dar I'll take a seat,
En ax fo' Booker T., you know,
    En res' my w'ary feet.

I'll tell him I has jis now 'rived,
    From ol' Virginny lan',
En took dat long en lonesom' drive
    To shake his willin' han'.

En dar I'll set en look at him,
    En he will look at me,
En fo' my eyes get dim,
    While I kin cl'erly see.

I'll take his gracious han'
    Widin my trimblin' grasp,
En praise de Lawd I reached de lan',—
    I's finished up my tas'.

" I's seen dis great, great cullered man,
    I's ready now to go;
You've done a great wuk in dis lan',
    Is why I lubs you so.''

So now my eyes I clos' to res',
    I's happy, yea, so free;
I's took de journey, stood de tes'
    En seen ol' Booker T.

Dedicated to Dr. W. H. Sheppard

[The returned missionary, who spent twenty years in Africa.]

On, on to the darkest continent,
    As the Adriatic sailed,
In Eighteen Hundred and Ninety,
    Many sad good-byes were wailed.

When two brave sons left their homes,
    Their kindred, yea their blood,
To wade in Africa's unknown,
    And overwhelming flood.

A caucasian and a negro,
    United heart and soul,
Bound for Ethiopia's soil,
    Yea Africa's distant goal.

As from the New York shore
    The steamer slowly starts,
Sheppard and Lapsley bade good-bye
    To sad but anxious hearts.

On, on, as the steamer glides,
    'Mid the rippling water's whirl,
On to the wild and savage land,
    The darkest in the world.

Yet, in that darkened land
    Were millions, yea unfed,
Who never had been told
    Of Christ the living bread.

But God had sent a message,
    To these men so brave,
To go in Ethiopia's land,
    And try these souls to save.

Gladly they heeded His command,
    To go 'mid danger and strife,
And work in that distant land,
    Yes, at the cost of life.

And so in Ethiopia's wild,
    These two men so brave,
Prayed for Ethiopia's child,
    Struggling a soul to save.

For weeks, yes, months they struggled,
    Working day and night,
Until at last, how happy, —
    There came a ray of light.

One soul had come to Christ,
    One made to understand,
The blessed Savior's voice,
    And heed to His command.

These leaders true and brave,
    Prayed to Him on high a prayer,
To thank Him for this blessing,
    And for His tender care.

But ere many months had passed.
    There came a sad, sad day,
A cloud o'er Africa's land was cast,
    For one had passed away.

A leader now was gone,
    One whom they did love,
Rev. Lapsley had been called
    To that home above.

His comrade also missed him,
    For he was left alone,
To dwell in Ethiopia's land,
    Afar from friends and home.

A work he had left unfinished,
    Which he had resolved to do,
But Sheppard decided by God's aid
    To carry the work on through.

So he started out one day,
    With Africa's savage band,
Determined to make his way
    To the Forbidden Land.*

Months they spent on the way,
    To carry a ray of light
To Heathen who knew no day,
    In a land where all was night.

After toiling daily,
    With Ethiopia's sons,
Many were brought to Christ,
    A victors crown was won.

They built a house of worship,
　　And toiled day after day,
Soon Ethiopia's sons
　　Had learned the narrow way.

They, too, began to preach,
　　And teach their fellowmen,
And for these blessings great
　　Their prayers did upward blend.

And in this land so dark,
　　Where never had been light,
The lame, in Christ, were made to walk.
　　The blind were given sight.

To Sheppard they gave great praise,
　　He'd ventured on their soil,
And Ethiopia's sons had raised
　　Thro' years of earnest toil.

For twenty years he struggled,
　　In Africa's darkened land,
Giving them the light
　　As they heeded his command.

Way off in Africa's land,
　　Let us in fancy look,
To see a heathen band,
　　Who'd never seen a book,—

Now preaching Christ and teaching,
　　With minds all free and bright,
All Hail to thee, oh Sheppard,
　　Who carried them the light.

A great work thou hast done,
　　To thee we give great praise,
Many laurels thou hast won
　　For thy remaining days.

---

*The Forbidden Land herewith mentioned has reference to a tribe
of savages in the interior, known as Bakubas.

De Wintah Styles

Come in, Aunt Jemima,
    Oh no, 'taint wof while,
I jis been out a lookin'
    At de wintah styles.

To see de change in coats,
    En how de hats will be,
To go into dem stores,
    La! 'tis a sight to see.

I jis stans' en looks,
    En den I looks en t'inks
What will be de next t'ing
    As we near de fashion's brink.

Case way back in my time,
    No sich styles as dese,
Ever cums befo' de folks, —
    We dressed den as we pleased.

We wo' our linsey frocks,
    En 'kerchiefs on our head,
En not dese great high hats,
    Heavy's eny lead.

But de styles dis day
    Am changed so from my time,
Eberyt'ing is gay,
    En hiferlutin fine.

De hats dey am so bery high,
    Wid feathers all aroun',
You can't tell what dey's made of,
    Or eben see de crown.

En chicken feathers, too,
    Dyed blue, red and green,
En folks wid hats a struttin'
    De same as eny queen.

De wimmen walkin' fru de streets,
  Wid diamon's in dey har,
En on dey hats ol' tuckey tails,
  A danglin' in de air.

Dey don't know de dif'rence,
  Fer dey struts en primp dey lips,
De same as dey was w'arin
  De fines' ostrich tips.

En coats like long jimswingers,
  Vest, too, like de men,
Dese wimmen all de money
  Dey kin git will spen'.

When dey husban's git de money,
  What I say you watch it,
De wimmen folks dey has it,
  Fo' he gits it in his pocket.

I'se lookin' fer de time to cum
  When dey will w'ar men's pants,
Dey's settin' back a lookin',
  En waitin' fer de chance.

Den de Lawd will say "enuf,"
  En take dem up on high,
Whar he kin set de fashions
  To rule dem in de sky.

Ambition

When e'er we enter Life's open field,
  Or life's duties are at hand,
When e'er to Necessity's voice we yield,
  Or heed to her just commands.

'Tis then we need that power,
  Which will aid us most in life,
And in every trying hour,
  Will serve to banish strife.

'Tis then we need to exercise,
    Those emotions of the soul,
Which will help us in our efforts rise
    And reach Life's distant goal.

'Tis then we need to cultivate,
    'Mid trying conditions,
Powers that will elevate
    As real ambition.

Ambition to help the old in life;
    Ambition to aid the young,
To lift from hovels, banish strife,
    And aid every one.

To be an aid in every task,
    And every petition,
As long as life shall last,
    Cultivate ambition.

Christmas Times

When are the children all happy and gay?
When do they ne'er grow tired of play?
When do their mouths seem like bells in chimes?
It is the merry Christmas times.

When do the little boys all get good?
And bring in coal and cut all the wood,
And every command of their parents mind,
'Tis just a week before Chistmas times.

That is the time when all of the work
Is done without a grumble or shirk.
The little boys then ne'er turn and twist,
When mother says, "Son, come here and do this."

Let the word be said, he's at her command,
Not once does he frown, or attempt to stand,
But goes at her bidding, happy and gay,
For it will soon be Christmas day.

And then old Santa, thro' all the snow,
Will come to those who've been good, you know;
Down the chimney he'll come and will not stop,
Till he fills each stocking full to the top.

When his task is o'er he takes his stand
Gazing at little ones in Dreamland,
Who in that land, all happy and gay,
Their minds all fixed on Christmas day.

And in a few hours, with merry hearts,
Little ones out of their warm beds dart,
All happy and gay, hearts full of cheer,
To see what's been bro't by Santa dear.

How happy is each little mind,
When every stocking full they find,
And presents scattered on the floor,
How could they ever ask for more?

No, no, but for many a year,
Christmas time to them will be dear,
And e'en in their prayers they make a pause
And ask many blessings on Santa Claus.

———————

De Men Folks ob Today

Ob all de subjicts I kin read,
    Or reason on so well,
De one I cum tonight to plead,
    Is de one I likes to tell.

'Tis all about dese men folks,
    Who's losin' all dey sense,
You needn't look at me and sneer,
    Case it's a lack fer common sense.

Dey's done los' all dey manners, too,
    En nebber rais' de hats,
Dis losin' sense, jis thrills me thru',
    Dey's wo's den eny chaps.

Why, when I was a comin' up,
　　En I aint so ol' as yit,
De men folks didn't seem sich bluffs,
　　En neber had sich fits,—

As de men folks ob today,
　　Puttin' on sich style,
In der hiferlutin' way,
　　Goodness, 'taint wof while.

Case when you courts de wimmen,
　　Dey don't lub you fo' yo' clo's,
Dat wud be a sinnin',
　　En ebery body knows.

Dey lubs you fo' yo' winnin' ways,
　　En not fo' dressin' fine,
Lub fo' clo's dese days don't pay,
　　Is what's been on my min'.

You stylish dudes who's settin' roun',
　　Ef you wants to marry,
Take off dem stylish frocks en gowns,
　　Use common sense, don't tarry.

Put on some good ol' wukin' clo's,
　　En git yo' se'f a job,
En don't be hangin' 'roun each day,
　　Wid some lazy mob.

You take dis good advice,
　　You, Dick, Tom en Harry,
En soon you'll hab a wife,
　　Ef you wants to marry.

De People's Literary

Well, well, you's cum at las'—
　　Cum in and hab dis seat;
Walkin's sich a tiresom' tas'
　　I'll fix a bite to eat.

It's been a week o'mo'
    Since I seed yo' lubely face;
En when I spied you at de do',
    Wid all dat hat en lace,—

I said it sho' is Mandy Lee,
    En my! but I was glad,
Till my po' heart did jump wid glee,
    As do a little lad.

Tell me, honey, whar's you bin,
    You sho' is lookin' sweet;
It seems as do de win'
    Jis blowed you off de street.

What makes you keep a singin',
    Why don't you answer me?
Yo' heart mus' be a ringin',
    Songs dat's full ob glee.

" Now, hush, Aunt Lou, you's makin fun,
    I ain't so awful fine,
But Jim West my heart has won,
    En dis here am de sign.''

He's gwine out to-night,
    To de People's Literary,
En tol' me look cle'n out ob sight
    En not to act contrary.

Ef you lubs me, Mandy Lee,
    Cum to de chu'ch to-night,
Lookin' purty as kin be,
    Yo' eyes all shinin' bri't.

When I looks at you dat night,
    Ef you greet me wid a smile,
You mean yo' lub is sho' alri't,
    I'll be one happy chile.

So I jis dressed to-night fo' him,
    Case he seems to lub me so,
I sholy do t'inks heaps ob him,
    But hates to tell him so.

So I'se gwine out to-night
    To sho' my lub is tru';
My heart is happy en so light,
    I don't know what to do.

En dat People's Literary,
    Am sumpin fine, fo' sho';
De chu'ch am always packed
    Way back to the do',

En when dey sing dem songs
    Yo' soul, it seems to rise,
Till you see de angel throngs
    Way up in de skies.

En when dey calls de roll
    Folks answer wid a speech,
'Twould tak' a 'mence big scroll
    To sum up what dey teach.

Dey sings de nices' songs
    You eber heahd befo',
I heahs dem all day long
    As I goes from do' to do'.

Dey makes big speeches, too,
    En dey soun' so bery high,
You'd t'ink dey's wrote by some one
    Dwellin' in de sky.

I jis can't tak' de time
    To tell de r'al good
Dese t'ings is on de min',
    En specs I neber cud.

But dis People's Literary
    I hopes may neber die;
En dat eben folks contra'y
    Will strive to make a try.

I specs to larn to speak en sing,
    En say big speeches, too,
To mak' dem chu'ch walls ring
    Lik' chimin' bells anew.

46

En when de part is bro't in,
    Mandy Lee's big name
Will shine among de res',
    Ringin' out wid fame.

You sho' will laf, but taint no use,
    I'll sho' be clos' behin'
When de People's Literary
    Stars begin to shine.

Superstitions

I ain't superstitious,
    But dis I sho' do know,
Dat ef a rooster walks his se'f up
    En crows right in y'o do',
Dar's sho' someone a comin'
    Say jis what you might,
Dar'll be a stranger at yo' hous'
    Fo' de cumin' ob de night.

I ain't superstitious,
    But dis I know is tru',
Say what you will, en do what you'll do;
    Ef yo' lef' han' itches,
You may t'nk it funny,
    But you sho' soon gwine er git
A little sum ob money.

I ain't superstitious,
    'Tis ignance I'll vow,
But sho's you're born,
    Dis is tru' some how,
Dat ef you starts a place,
    En has to turn back,
En fo'gits to make a cross,
    En spit right in yo' track,

Some bad luck sho' will follow,
    Dis t'ing sho' is tru',
Ef you don't believe me,
    I tell you what to do:
Jis go some whar fo' fun,
    En den turn back to see,
Some bad luck sho' will follow,
    'Tis tru' as it kin be.

I ain't superstitious,
    But I tell you what I've seen,
Ef you eats at a table
    Whar dar's jis thirteen,
You min' what I say,
    As sho's dar's a sky
One ob dat thirteen
    Will be sho to die.

I ain't superstitious
    But here's annoder fact,
En dis t'ing sho is tru'
    No matter whar you's at,
Dat if you starts a place
    En a black cat crosses you
'Tis sho en sartin bad luck
    No matter what you do.

I can't be superstitious
    En sho I ain't to blame
But if you cum in one do' ob de hous'
    En don't go out de same
Your min', it sho is bad luck,
    You kin turn dis way en dat
But bad luck sho will follow
    No matter whar you's at.

I ain't superstitious
    But some t'ings I do know,
Ef you sweeps yo' hous' out arter dark
    'Tis bad luck fo' you sho,

En please don't spill no salt,
    It jis as sho is tru'
Dat sumpin's gwine to happen,
    Min' what I say, too.

I ain't superstitious
    But I tell you fus en las'
It sho is awful luck
    To break a lookin' glass;
Bad luck fo' seven years
    Is de title read;
Dat sho is one t'ing dat I fears —
    One t'ing dat I dread.

I ain't superstitious
    But dis ain't no lie,
Ef a bird flies in de hous'
    Dars some one gwine to die;
'Tis jis as true as it kin be
    En when you see de bird
Some one's gwine to leabe dat hous',
    Case die am de word.

I ain't superstitious
    But let yo' lef' eye quiver,
Trouble sho will follow,
    You jis well 'gin to shiver;
En let yo' lef' foot itch
    'Tis jis as tru' fo' sho,
You jis well pack yo' satchel,
    Case on strange lan' you mus' go.

I ain't superstitious,
    But dis I sho do know,
In de ebening arter dark
    Ef you hears a rooster crow
Hasty news am cumin,
    'Tis tru' as it kin be,
En you jis well wa'r a long face
    En set en wait to see.

I ain't supersitious,
    It's ign'ance, 'tis a fact;
It jis sho's, too,
    Dat fo' 'telligence you lack,
But when settin at de table,
    La sakes! don't sneeze,
It's a sho sign ob death,
    Say what you please.

I ain't superstitious
    En eberybody knows
Dat I ain't superstitious
    Eny whar I goes,
But y'all sho kin tell
    En read between de lines,
I ain't superstitious
    But I do beliebe in signs.

Poet of Our Race

[Dedicated to the memory of Paul Laurence Dunbar.]

Oh, Poet of our Race,
    We reverence thy name
As thy hist'ry we retrace,
    Which enfolds thy widespread fame.

We loved thee, yea, too well,
    But He dids't love thee more
And called thee up with Him to dwell
    On that Celestial shore.

Thy sorrows here on earth,
    Yea, more than thou coulds't bear,
Burdened thee from birth
    E'en in their visions fair.

And thou, adored of men,
    Whose bed might been of flowers,
With mighty stroke of pen
    Expressed thy sad, sad hours.

Thou hast been called above,
    Where all is peace and rest,
To dwell in boundless love,
    Eternally and blest.

And, yet, thou still dost linger near,
    For thy words, as sweetest flowers,
Do grow in beauty 'round us here
    To cheer us in sadest hours.

Thy thoughts in rapture seem to soar
    So far, yea, far above,
And shower a heavy downpour
    Of sparkling, glittering love.

Thou, with stroke of mighty pen,
    Hast told of joy and mirth,
And read the hearts and souls of men
    As cradled from their birth.

The language of the flowers,
    Thou hast read them all,
And e'en the little brook
    Responded to thy call.

All Nature hast communed
    And lingered, yea, with thee,
Their secrets were entombed
    But thou hast made them free.

Oh, Poet of our Race,
    Thou dost soar above ;
No paths wilt thou retrace
    But those of peace and love.

Thy pilgrimage is done,
    Thy toils on earth are o'er,
Thy victor's crown is won,
    Thou'lt rest forever more.

To Professor Byrd Prillerman

[President of West Virginia Colored Institute.]

Dar's a skool in West Virginny,
    Dat I hears dem call de Farm,
Whar dey raises ebery t'ing to eat,
    En has de bigges' barns,—
Whar de ho'ses en de cows,
    In restin' spend de night,
And w'ar away de hours,
    To dey own heart's delight.

'Tis dar dey teaches eberyt'ing
    In de wuken line,
As much as folks kin well take in
    Upon de common min';
Dey l'arns you how to cook,
    Dey l'arns you how to sew;
In fact, dey teaches eberyt'ing
    Dat you wants to know.

Has you eber seed de president
    Ob dat skool, de Farm?
De man who bosses eberyt'ing,
    From de skool room to de barn;
I tell you he's a great man,
    To meet him you kin see
De 'telligence beamin' from his face
    As blossoms from a tree.

He's hammered on de chillun's heads,
    Fo', lo, dese thirty years,
Poundin' knowledge in dem
    'Mid dumbness en 'mid fears;
He's bro't dem from de dunce stool
    Ob ignance en disgrace,
En trained dem in his skool
    To lead folks ob de race.

He's one de oldes' teachers,
    In West Virginny State,
En what dat man don't know
    Ain't worthy to relate ;
So, when you wants to go to skool
    To be sho to l'arn,
Go to dat Cullered Institute
    Dat some folks call de Farm.

Sister Johnson's Speech

I went to chu'ch, 'tother night,
De silvah moon was shinin' bright ;
Brudder Johnson en his wife was dar,
Dey went wif Jane en me en ma.

Sister Johnson, she jumped up to speak,
She said dat sinners ought to seek
To git the 'ligon ob de soul
Dat shined out in dem bright as gol'.

She said dat sinners ob dis day
Tho't so ob dress en looked so gay
Dat when it cum de Lawd to seek
Dey hearts and souls was pow'ful weak.

En, too, so Sister Johnson said,
De Lawd He am de staff en bread ;
He feeds de soul, en fills it, too,
En makes you eber feel anew.

She said, you little gals en boys
Who sets in chu'ch en makes a noise,
You needs to come into de fol'
En git de 'ligon ob de soul.

You needs to fix yo' soul up new,
You better min' what I say, too,
You frisky little gals and boys,
Who likes to set and make a noise.

Sister Johnson she speaked what she know'd
Case she has trabbled on de road,
En speaked to folk in crowded hous',
Where chillun set jis like a mouse.

She's speaked to folks in cities, too,
En towns en villages a few ;
She tol' dem 'bout dey low disgrace
En tried to raise folks ob de race.

She says she means to set a zample
En gibe you folks a little sample
Ob how to serve de Lawd outright,
In mornin' or de darkes' night.

De Lawd He made de shinin' moon
To light you fru dis worl' ob gloom ;
He made de sun to shine fru day
En light you on de narrow way.

He made dis worl' so cle'r en bright,
He made de darkness ob de night ;
He made de grass to look so green
En de snow dat 'pears so white and clean.

En, brudders, as I now do speak,
My voice am gitten low en weak,
But I hopes my talk will be a blessin'
En dat from it you'll l'arn a lesson.

En as I goes from place to place,
I'll try to raise folks from disgrace,
En soun' my notes in cleares' tones,
Befor' I takes de train fer home.

I'll let dem know I takes my stan'
Fer 'spectability ob de lan'
En ef dey still keeps on der ways,
A mighty fog I specs to raise.

James Hugo Johnston

On a hill near Petersburg,
    Facing the old historic town,
There lives a model Negro—
    One who's won renown.

A man we should be proud of—
    President of a school ;
He holds full sway in his modest way,
    Of reserved and dignified rule.

'Tis just such men the world needs,
    One whose record stands
Unblemished by a darkened deed,
    Clear, wavering thro' the land.

Live on, thou brave and honored sire,
    That many thy paths may retrace,
To keep them from the deepened mire
    Of folly and disgrace.

Live on, thou noble son of Ham—
    On, on, thro life's rugged ways ;
With steps clear and unfaltering,
    Deserving of thy praise.

The Strawberry

At first we see the tiny leaves
And no one at their coming grieves,
But watch so eager each day and hour
For the coming of the little flower.

Each day, then, to the strawberry bed
The feet of little ones do tread
And around the bed they gather soon,
Watching for the strawberry bloom.

The little blossoms so sweet and small
They watch until each petal falls ;
How happy they feel, then ; oh, how merry,
When they find the first strawberry.

Happier beings were never seen
As they gaze on the little berry green,
With happy hearts and faces strange,
Wondering when it's color will change.

After a few days shall have passed
Still resuming their daily task
To the strawberry bed again they tread
To see who can find a strawberry red.

And as they find them, how happy at heart,
As strawberries in their little mouths dart ;
Romping about, full of frolic and glee,
With little mouths full as they can be.

Soon they leave the strawberry bed
After eating all the berries red,
Thanking God, and Heaven above,
For the little berries that they love.

As We Sow We Shall Reap

As we go about the toils of life,
As we witness each day, it's burdens and strife,
Thinking not of days of the future or past,
Knowing not where in life our lots may be cast, —

'Tis then in life's broad and fertile field,
In tho'tlessness to fate we yield ;
Not deeming it wise our tho'ts to cast
On any works or deeds of the past.

Still tho'tlessly we struggle along
Amid Life's great and fearless throng ;
Thro' darkened caves, o'er rugged steeps,
Thinking not that as we sow we reap.

But later on, when years have flown,
And of life's cares we've weary grown,
'Mid silence, tho'ts in our minds do creep,
That as we've sown, we now do reap.

We think of our heavy burdens and cares,
It seems to us more than we can bear ;
It pains our heart, we utter a groan,
Yet, we're reaping what we have sown.

Oh, if we only could blot out the past,
And e'en it's memory in some sea cast,
Oh, could we but live this life again,
Such burdens would not on our minds remain.

But now our eyes are dim with age,
We near the last line of life's page,
We'll seal it's contents with a groan, —
Reaping—reaping what we have sown.

Before your eyes grow dim with age,
You, who are on Life's busy stage,
Each day you labor, do mindful keep,
That as you sow you will surely reap.

What's de Use ob Wukin in de Summer Time at All

What's de use ob wukin in de Summer time at all,
When de sun am bilin' hot en de sweat begins to fall ;
What's de use ob diggin' in de fields ob co'n en 'taters,
Plantin' squash en beans en pickin' ripe tomaters.

What's de use ob pickin' in de field's ob huckleberries,
Or pullin' at de trees, pickin' off de cherries ;
What's de use ob wukin or plowin' in de heat,
Eatin' ha'f-cooked meals en blisterin' yo' feet.

What's de use ob habin houses in de summer time,
'Tis plenty good out doors when de blessed sun do shine ;
When de fields is clothed wid green, de meadow en de lane,
You need no kin' ob shelter 'cept in fallin' ob de rain.

'Tis mighty hard a wukin when de sun am beamin' down
En not a spot ob coolness to be seen aroun',
When ebery way you turn, de sun am shinin' hot,
En ebery inch ob flesh am a bu'nin' spot.

'Tis mighty hard a walkin' in fields ob turned up groun',
For miles en miles a plantin', out ob hearin' ob de town,
A sowin' ob de wheat or plantin' ob de co'n ;
It sho is bitter meat en hard wuk sho's you born.

'Tis fearful hard a-stayin' in de field de livelong day,
When de hours am slowly passin' en you hab so long to
            stay ;
En you wuk so bery hard when you stop you hardly know
De way to take fer home dat wont seem kin' o' slow.

But arter t'inkin' ober all de change is got to cum,
I spec's I'll take de Summer, wid all de shinin' sun ;
Case when de winter sets his foot upon dis naked earf,
He brings about much sadness to take de place of mirf.

Den de hard times cum a peepin' en a movin' in fer sho,
Sho'in' ob his grinnin' teeth, knockin' at yo' do' ;
'Tis den he tries to rob yo' ob trunk en clo's,
En soon you fin' yo'se'f a-settin' out ob do's.

De chills dey soon cum ober you, you fin'no whar to go,
As you wander 'long about de street en seek from do' to do';
No wuk to do, no shelter, not a crus' ob bread to eat,
No good warm clo's to sooth' de chill, no shoes fer naked
            feet.

'Tis den I see de use ob wukin in de sun,
It matters not how hot, no day I'll eber shun ;
'Tis den I see de need ob plantin' wheat en co'n,
En puttin' up fer winter, 'tis a fact, as sho's you born.

'Tis den I know de need ob drappin' squash en 'taters,
Plantin' beets, en plantin' beans en pickin' ripe tomatoes ;
'Tis den I see de good old need ob pickin' huckleberries,
En pullin' down de limbs a-gatherin' ob de cherries.

For all dis helps, I tells you, when Winter cums wid col',
En starts His round ob freezin' en starvin' many souls ;
It keeps away old hunger when He cums wid starin' face,
En leabes you a sufferin' en starvin' in disgrace.

En now I'll tell you one en all, de Summer time am hot,
I'd sooner be a little warm den freezin' 'bout in spots ;
I'd radder be out in de field when de sun an beamin' down,
En wuk de blisters on my hand as I make a weary round.

I'll take ol' Summer any time on my list fer sho,
Den fool wid winter in His wrath when He knocks upon
                de do' ;
I'll take de heat en sweat en plant de fields ob co'n,
Radder'n face ol' Winter's breff in de coolness ob de morn.

No day will eber 'pear so long, no field so bu'nin' hot,
But what I'll plant de c'on en fill in ebery spot ;
No idle moments will I spar' but days ob earnest toil,
To sho de blessed benefits ob wukin in de soil.

Case Summer time to me am dear en 'tis den I spec's to wuk
En ef I has de time to spar' 'tis Winter time I'll shirk ;
I'll try to 'scape His freezin' days en b'ar me burdens free,
Take Winter time in all His ways but Summer time fer me.

The Lost Teddy Bear

Well, Teddy, I have found you,
    It's been one week to-day
Since I missed you, Teddy dear,
    While in the yard at play.

I wandered far and wide,
  And knew not where to go
To find you, Teddy, dear,
  But, oh, I missed you so.

I know some naughty boy
  Stole you, dear, from me,
And if I only knew
  Who that boy could be, —

I'd scold him, yes, I'd scold him,
  And I'll just bet he'd not dare
To interfere again
  With my dear little Teddy bear.

And, oh, you were so nice and clean,
  One would scarcely know
That you were the same little Teddy
  Lost one week ago.

But still I welcome you, my dear,
  And will wash you nice and clean
And try forget that you were lost
  And believe it all a dream.

So, again I embrace you, Teddy,
  For I love you just the same,
And tho' you look so dirty,
  'Twas the boy, you ain't to blame.

Meal Time

Liza! call dat chile
  En make her wash her face
En cum on to de table
  So Pap can say de grace.

You let de chillun hab der ways
  And soon dey'll manage you,
Ef you don't try to check dem,
  Come on, Bob en Sue!

Yo'all set up to de table,
    'Twill take a ha'f a day
To get y'all to yo' meals,
    Cumin in dat way.

Don't make sich noise wid dem stools !
    Does you hear me, Jane ?
Ef 'twarn't fer we ol' folks
    You chillun wud raise Cain.

Set up straight dar, Jimbo !
    We all is ready, Pap !
Stop dat whisperin' Lisha !
    En pull off dat air cap.

Yo' all cud'n sho keep still
    'Till Pap cud say de grace ;
I don't know what's gwine to cum
    Ob dis young cullud race.

Sal ! git de spoon en git mo' hash—
    Don't spill it on de flo';
Take up all de co'n cakes,
    I t'ink Pap wants some more.

Abe, don't stuff yo' mouf so full,
    You sho kin git some mo' ;
Be kerful wid dat buttermilk—
    Don't spill it on de flo'.

En pass de cakes aroun',
    Don't t'ink all 'bout yo' self ;
Try to l'arn some manners,
    You ugly little elf.

You kids done eat enuf !
    Git up from dat table
En clean dem dishes up
    As fas' as you is able.

En you sweep de kitchen good,
    Be quick about it, too ;
'Twill be time fer anodder meal,
Befo' you chaps git thro'.

Dedication Day

[Read at the dedication of the new Mt. Zion Baptist Church, Staunton, Va.]

What means this vast assemblage here,
    Of people great and grand,
Who've come to us from afar and near,
    At the heed of one's command.

Why come ye to Mt. Zion's walls,
    Ye folks in grand array ?
''We've heeded to the pastor's call,
    'Tis Dedication Day.''

List ! hear ye not those songs,
    Which pour forth streams of love ?
It seems that some angelic throng
    Has sent them from above.

Why are these souls with music stirred,
    What means all this, I pray ?
Can it be you haven't heard,
    'Tis Dedication Day ?

The work of a hand is finished,
    The toil of a day is done,
One's labor is diminished,
    Yet a great work to be done.

We stand 'mid beauty and splendor,
    And gaze on these sacred walls,
While our hearts many thanks do tender,
    To Him who dost heed our calls.

You've struggled, yea, toiled unceasing,
    To complete a glorious work,
Each day new efforts increasing,
    Daring not shrink nor shirk.

Part of your toils are at an end,
    And part, yea, just begun,
As your feeble efforts blend,
    In love to the Holy One.

And now you have assembled here,
    'Mid efforts good and great,
With happy hearts, minds full of cheer,
    A gift to dedicate.

To dedicate, means to give to God,
    And may He who inspires us to live
And trod each day earth's lowly sod,
    Instill in us power to give.

And as we our minds in holiness lift,
    We offer to Him above,
A sacred, yea, a noble gift,
    In high honor of His love.

For 'twas He who gave you power
    To erect this building grand,
A monument to tower,
    A glory to this land.

Let all unite in these songs,
    Yea, your feeble voices lift,
And help this mighty throng,
    To dedicate this glft.

And thank your God above
    For the true-hearted leader sent ;
He's led seven years in love,
    Calling sinners to repent.

He's toiled for Mt. Zion's daughters and sons
    That they might a true people be,
That they live in love to the Holy One,
    Has been his prayer and constant plea.

'Tis Moses He sent to lead you,
    That you heed His gentle command,
He'll lead you safely thro',
    Till you've reached the promised land.

A man inspired by God,
    He a noble work has done ;
He'll reap his just reward,
    When the harvest time has come.

And to Mt. Zion's daughters and sons
    I pray that your life may be,
An emblem of the Holy One,
    From strife and malice free.

And may the good Savior above,
    Bless this congregation great,
As they in prayers and songs of love,
    This building dedicate.

And to all who've helped in the cause,
    You've won for yourself renown ;
I pray you abide in His laws,
    He'll add many stars to your crown.

Autobiography
and Poems

MRS. HENRY LINDEN
Springfield, Ohio

AUTOBIOGRAPHY

I was born September 22, 1859, under the British government in Canada, fourteen miles from London, and lived there to the age of eight, when my parents brought me to the states. We first went to Kentucky, Campbell county, where my grandfather lived at that time—my father's old home place.

My father was born in slavery. He ran away before the war, when only a boy, and went to Canada, where of course he obtained his freedom.

My mother was a Canadian. She had a good English education and taught school, and when my father went back to Kentucky it was a brand new thing to see a negro teacher, and it did not set very well with the rebels in those days, so they ordered my father to take his family and leave Kentucky; but as slavery was over and he was free he thought that he had a right to live where he pleased, and declined to go. However, in a short time we were compelled to go to save our lives, as those rebels were preparing to burn us out. The powder had been placed under the house during the absence of our family on Sunday, and every arrangement was made to burn us out, but one of the gang weakened and turned state's evidence. That was all that saved us.

So then we left Kentucky and came to Ohio, where we have remained ever since. We first went out on a farm two miles from Richmond, Ohio, where we remained for two years (Lockland, Ohio). Then my father obtained a good position as foreman for two real estate men. As he was not a scholar and could not write, the responsibilities became too much for him and he lost his mind, becoming melancholy; he was perfectly harmless, but could do no business.

At that time there were several small children, and as I was the eldest, although not yet twelve years old, it became necessary for me to go to work to help support the family and earn a living for myself. Of course I had very little schooling. I had to stop school and begin the hardships of life. I soon got a place to nurse, and while I was nursing I was the cook occasionally, so therefore I learned to cook so well that when I was there six months the cook became sick and I took her place. I was then not thirteen years old. After that time I continued to cook, but my father's health grew worse and we had to leave the town and go to the country, where he grew able to work a little on the farm. With my help and a younger brother's assistance we did very well that year. I made a good farm hand, and was glad to work and help my parents.

My father grew worse again, and hearing of the Delaware springs at Delaware, Ohio, we thought the water might help him, so we moved to Delaware. The water did him good, and I think added a great many years to his life. I continued cooking at very good wages.

Soon a Chinaman came to the town and opened a laundry. He advertised for help, making good offers to induce girls to learn the trade. I went there to work with several other girls, all were white but me. Of course my girl friends laughed at me and often called me "Chinaman," and I would feel bad, but knew that I was doing the best that I could; I took it for my share. I learned at eleven years of age to trust God; though young I believed he would bring me out more than conqueror, and he did. Some of those that laughed at me had to come to me for work when I opened my laundry, but I could not hire them because they did not understand the work. Now when I first learned the trade this Chinaman hired me to iron and polish and gave me a dollar a day; I worked with him until he moved his laundry to Columbus, Ohio, and was the only one working there that learned the trade thoroughly. The trade is a profound secret with the Chinese. They will pretend to teach you, but if you are not pretty sharp you will never learn. I found that out at once and began to take advantage of every available opportunity, and would make starch at home and try it by ironing a shirt. I also took some of the chemical that he used in his starch and had it analyzed so as to learn what it was made of, for I made up my mind to some day keep a laundry of my own, and have since done so and was very successful.

My dear readers, I tell this hoping that some young girl will profit by my experience. I will give you a brief sketch of my life to the present time.

My home being of such an humble nature and I had to live so poorly and was not very strong, I married at the age of seventeen, and was very unfortunate in getting a husband who was unkind and did not support me; he was everything but a husband to me. I married against my parents' will, so I thought as I had made my bed hard I would do the best I could and would not annoy them any more than I could help; so I again went out to service to make a living, with a strong determination to make life a success. Discouraging it seemed that those whom I had thought were my friends proved to be enemies.

I lived with my first husband nearly two years. He proved to be a gambler and blackleg of the very worst type, so I thought I was lucky to leave with my life. He would sell my clothes when he would get broke, and the furniture out of the house when I would be out at work, to obtain money to gamble with. I was young and foolish, and when he would come and plead with me to forgive him I would, and work and get more things; but at last I tired of that life, and one day I came home from my work at a late hour only to find my furniture gone and all my clothes sold again, and he was not in sight, nor did he return until the wee hours of the morning. When he came I, tired and worn out with a hard day's work, was lying on a straw tick that he had left, without any cover, but the weather was warm. I will always believe that he intended to take my life, for when he came he brought another man who had just got out of the penitentiary, and was a desperate character. I called the neighbors next door, and the villian left, but my so-called husband remained, and I vowed that morning that I was through with him. As I had my living to make I would make it alone in peace.

He went from bad to worse until he died, but before his death he married a white woman and she grew as tired of him as I did. I obtained a divorce from him, and after I applied he went to the penitentiary for stealing.

I worked right along, and the people I worked for were kind to me and tried every way to console me, and I never lost hope for the future, always believing that I would make my life count for something and be a credit to my race, as I have tried to live right and set a good example for the young, and asked God to guide me. I do not mean to say that I am perfect, for none of us are without fault, but have tried to do the best I could in my weakness. I have had a hard time, as everyone has that has had to struggle for a living at all kinds of work.

In time I had the opportunity to go to Florida as a cook,

and while there met and married a gentleman who at the time was in the detective service—a railroad detective—and made his mark in the service, but was a regular spendthrift, and spent money faster than he made it, so that made me work hard again, but this time engaged in business for myself. I opened a laundry and later learned the French cleaning, and of these two trades I have made a success in life. After I had learned my trade as a cleaner I had just fifty cents to start my business with, but in six years that fifty cents made me four thousand dollars that I could see. My work was altogether for actresses and transient trade at the hotels, so the hotels and theatres have proved a blessing to me. Today I am worth several thousand dollars, living well and doing a first-class business. This is told to help some one else who may have my experience or one just as hard.

When I was forty-two years old I became very active in club work; although belonging to clubs for ten years was too busy to take any part in the work, but for five years have been an active worker. Am a member of six clubs and president of two of them. The clubs of which I am president are the Phyllis [*sic*] Wheatley and the Friday Afternoon Study Club. The Phyllis Wheatley has adopted an orphan child, a little girl, and support her and expect to educate her if she lives. The Friday Club has under consideration a day nursery and kindergarten for colored children, for which we are working to that end and hope to accomplish in time, to the credit of the race. All the other clubs are for charity and self-improvement.

Five years ago we took up needlework in the Wednesday Afternoon Club, and I learned that art, and in that time have made nearly 250 pieces of doilies, center-pieces, pillow-shams, standcovers, sideboard and dresser scarfs, and many smaller pieces. Also have the honor of bringing the first doily to the State Federation. Our president asked the ladies to bring some fancy work, and I was the only one who responded.

The club work has been very helpful to me, and since that time I have been inspired to write poetry. In January, 1905, I wrote my first lines; subject, "Tell Her So," and since that time have written forty or fifty poems. When I had written fourteen pieces I put them in print in pamphlet form and named them "Scraps of Time," selling them to the public at twenty-five cents each, and in four months sold over five hundred of them, and am now preparing for this book. I have contributed my poems to magazines and to the daily papers in my city and abroad. I contribute now to a white newspaper, the Daily News, the people's paper in our city with the largest circulation. It is a white paper, but they print my poems and run my cut as well.

Now, dear readers, the reason I am giving you a little sketch of my life is to show you what you can do if you will. With push, pluck and ambition and Christ as your leader, you will make life a success. Now I am going to add my poems to this book.

I have two lovely boys, and believe that they will make great men if they live.

I have a good, kind husband. This is my third one, and he is old enough for my father. He was born a slave and fought in the Civil War, with no opportunity for schooling, but with all of his disadvantages he is a successful business man, and he does the largest transfer business in Springfield, Ohio. He has been married before and raised a creditable family of children. He was a widower for nine years previous to his marriage to me.

My second husband died after a long spell of sickness, and

left me with two baby boys. We were buying a home, and I was five hundred dollars in debt on it when he died, without a dollar on earth only that I worked for. Now you may imagine my position; two children, one three years old and the other five months. It took nerve and ambition to assume the responsibility, but I trusted God and came out all right. He opened different avenues in life for me. I did a paying business and was very successful. I had to keep a girl to care for my children while working at my trade. I was a widow only one year, and in that time got out of debt and bought a horse and buggy; so my circumstances were very good when I married my third husband. But he was in hard luck. He had been well fixed, but had lost it all by bad management, though I have never regretted marrying him. He is a good, kind husband and an ideal step-father. My boys fairly worship him and he does them.

My husband is a very useful man. He is an inventor, and has invented several useful articles that are in use today and giving satisfaction. The Linden piano truck, that is used by almost every transfer man and piano store in Ohio, is his invention; also a piano lamp that is in use, a hose union, and the window curtain rollers that are used in almost every home in the world. But with all his inventions and patent rights he has profited very little, as he sold them all at a sacrifice. Some one else is making the money out of them; he is only getting the honor of the name. He has been in the transfer business for forty years, and is now making a success at that. We both know the art of starting with nothing and making life a success. We know what it is to toil hard day and night to make ends meet.

Now, dear readers, I tell you these things to encourage you through life; to show you if you have the will power and pride and ambition you will be victorious in whatever you undertake, and do not get the idea that everything is against you, for God is no respector of persons, and man is just what he wills to be. The world is here and you must grasp every opportunity and never think any position too high for you to fill. Think more of yourself than anyone else, and have faith in your own ability, and believe that you can do what others have done, and when you are in the right just stand to fight and conquer if it kills. Though wrong puts on a stronger coat, and often shows up fight, when the battle is ended it always favors right.

I write a brief sketch of my life to inspire others so that they take advantage of passing opportunities. Our young should be encouraged. Instead of scolding and finding fault with them, let us who are mothers encourage the young to look up and not be content with so little. Let us teach our boys that to be men of note they must be self-supporting and take care of their families with the dignity of any race or people; and also teach them if, when married, they cannot get what is needed in their homes without denying themselves, to remember that it is manly to see the family provided for if they have to sacrifice themselves. The thing we need is more manly men and more noble women who will stand up for the right, never faint or fall, and whose great abilities will demand respect from all. We live in an age of prosperity, with everything at our command if we will just keep on moving as we should, hand in hand.

Little did I think five years ago that the world would be reading after me, with such a limited schooling, but today the greatest men and women of my own race and others are reading my works, in this country and the old country, and giving me great praise for my ambition and helpful efforts.

The president of our own America as well as kings and rulers of the old country is applauding my work with loud praises. It is worth while to do something. What need you care for the would-be critics that are doing nothing themselves and criticize your efforts? Take new courage and "pull for the shore." My efforts were criticized, but what did I care for that. I started with that expectation, but with God as my leader I expected to win the fight in the end.

> Dare to be true, dare to do right,
>   With Christ as your leader
> You will win the fight.

FOR THE GOOD
OF THE PYTHIAN ORDER

For the good of the order it behooves me to say
That the supreme lodge of Pythians has set apart this day
As an annual thanksgiving in a religious way;
We must return thanks to God for his goodness.

We appreciate the fact and do not take it back,
That we make rapid growth and improve every year;
The joy and comfort of doing what is right
Overbalances sorrow and care, and today we are prosperous and
    happy.

This organization has something of which to boast,
It stands above all others this side of the coast,
For the support of its widows and orphans this lodge does the
    most
That I know, for I've tested its treasures.

Its laws are all right and right up to date,
But like all other good things it sometimes meets fate

In unlawful members, and they go on at such a rate
It almost takes a regiment to get them straight,

But our people are learning that law must be obeyed,
That they can no longer stand in the way;
They must be gotten rid of and go out to stay,
For this is for the good of the order.

Now, dear sisters, you must have minds of your own,
Not to let ignorant men lead you wrong,
And when you are ditched they will laugh and sing you a song,
"I'm sorry; you should have known better,"

But look at your law and be governed by that,
Be united as Calanthians and take a stand
That you will run your order without the help of a man;
Confide in each other—this is a good plan to have a creditable
    order.

Let us this coming year live as we should,
Each one endeavoring to make their word good,
And set a good example to those we may hood,
Then the courts will all grow and prosper.

As women of our race let us look up to God
For his blessings and trust in his word
And on our thanksgiving be of one accord,
And then we will be prosperous and happy.

TO THE WHEEL OF PROGRESS

Your name is the Wheel of Progress—a pleasant name indeed,
Move on in line of progress, for that is what we need,
The things that lead to progress are what we do and say and mean,
We can have a world of progress if we use this term and theme.

Now to the Wheel of Progress so cultured and refined,
With noble thought and action, with able brain and mind,

Women of different callings and teachers of different schools,
We feel to acknowledge you our leaders as a rule.

Much depends on you for the future and the coming generations
    at lodge,
Your teachings and grand example, though sometimes it may seem
    hard,
Will bring laurels to crown your efforts
When you go home to meet our Lord.

And we appreciate you; yes, more than tongue can tell.
With Mrs. Jones as president we know you will do well,
With your various departments—charity, literary and art—
We expect at the next Federation to hear from you a grand report.

I have a sweet recollection of the first poem I ever wrote,
Was read by Miss Hetty Taylor, that inspired me to be a poet,
And of course your club I will always love for its loyalty to me;
That proves that you believe in progress, so that encouraged me.

May long live the Wheel of Progress, and in history may her
    name be found,
When her members' toils are ended and their labors have been
    crowned,
I hope she will leave a record that will live and last;
So sweet will be the memory when looking back over the last.

Let us build a monument in something that will live when we are
    gone,
That may year after year grow brighter, that time will not
    crumble down,
That coming generations may look on it with pride,
Then you will prove a blessing as club women true and tried.

But may the gem that we make be lasting and grow as the days
    roll on,
And glitter instead of tarnish until it becomes as bright as the sun,
And coming generations will prosper from your well trained hands
And honor the Wheel of Progress all over this broad land.

THE Y. M. C. A.

One of our race's greatest needs in this country today
Is a number of well supported and managed Y. M. C. A.;
Yes, in every city and town and hamlet around
Where the feet of our race treads over the ground.

Our young men need pleasure in various ways
As well as hard labor and study all day,
And there is no better place for them to be
Than in some well equipped and well managed Y. M. C. A.

And let us be awakened to the needs of today,
And make a sacrifice to support our Y. M. C. A.,
Then our young men will have some place to play
Simple games, and read good literature at the Y. M. C. A.

If we would have creditable men we must rear creditable boys,
Give them every advantage that will add to their morals,
And let us remember in this enlightened day
These things can all be found in the Y. M. C. A.

As mothers of a race we must do as well as say,
And make a strong effort to help the Y. M. C. A.
Let the church be first to teach them to say,
"I am a loyal member of the Y. M. C. A."

Now to the credit of our race we have today
In the city of Springfield a Y. M. C. A.,
With Springfield's bad name, its riot and shame,
We have something to be proud of then—Y. M. C. A.

Let us resolve in our hearts that we as a race
Will do all we can in our power to replace
The good name of Springfield to the credit of our race,
By indorsing every good move with the Y. M. C. A.

Now for my part I am here to say
That I will do my whole duty by the Y. M. C. A.

You can do as you please, but God blesses me,
And I will make it my business to help the Y. M. C. A.

BRAVE MAN AND BRAVE WOMAN

Brave man and brave woman,
With brave and honest heart,
And with their money will not part,
Will make life a grand success.

I know what it is to labor hard;
And with pluck and ambition
And womanly brain I ventured out
And aspired to learn a trade.

Of laundress and French cleaning
I learned the trade, worked hard,
And strict attention to business paid,
And found it worth while to learn a trade,

If you have no wealth, don't be sad,
Take if for your lot, don't think it bad,
But strive for the front with honest heart,
And exercise your brains and hands—
You will find this is a very good plan.

ALL WE ASK IS JUSTICE

The National Federation is a grand and glorious band
Of noble colored women that invades this land;
They've taken a grand stand in making a demand
For their offsprings of this land justice.

CHORUS:

Hurrah! Hurrah! You will hear our voices ring;
Hurrah! Hurrah! You will hear our women sing
When they have fought the battle

That has won the glorious prize
That we have been fighting for so long called justice.

We are making a great sacrifice, but mean to win the prize,
Makes no difference what it costs us we mean to live and try
To make the future better or we will know the reason why—
The only thing we are asking now is justice.

We will let the awful past alone and act as we call wise,
We are willing to work hard and make any sacrifice
Or do anything we can to help our race to rise,
But all we ask at any hands is justice.

We feel that we are right in making this demand;
Our fathers worked and shed their blood and made this country
      grand,
They have fought in every battle and are willing yet to stand,
And all they ask this country now is justice.

But we feel at last we have a friend in Roosevelt the president;
He stands for right, a hero bold, as he knows all races have a
      soul;
As chief executive of this land he makes this stern and last
      demand,
And means it, too—for every man justice.

As women of Ohio state we ask each state to federate,
And this will make us stronger; when every state is organized,
And all are fighting for this prize, you will hear
Our women cry, "We must have justice."

AS WOMEN OF OUR RACE

As women of our race we have the odds to face
In battling for our rights;
But we will take it for our share,

Never murmur, never fear,
Through God we will win the fight.

God is opening doors for us,
And bids us enter in and be his guest
In many a walk of life
That was closed to us through strife
By the more favored race.

Now we may win the fight by being loyal,
By training minds and hands,
As mothers of this land
To show their grit and sand
By working hard.

Then we will demand a place
Side by side with any race
In this broad land;
Let us prepare to fill a place
Through ambition, dignity and grace.

ENCOURAGEMENT

Encouragement is what I need, encouraged I ought to be,
Encouragement from one like you is all and all to me;
I like to speak encouraging to any one I meet,
I feel encouraged when I do, for they encourage me.

We are here to encourage anything that is right;
God intends it thus to be, and we will win a home
That will not fade whenever we cross life's sea,
Let us remember that encouragement belongs to God's great plan

Of making pilgrims happy while traveling through this land—
Then why not be encouraged when looking o'er the past
And know it is better farther on,
And reward will come at last.

THE FALL IS HERE

The fall is here, with its brown leaves falling
And its cold night winds kissing the flowers;
Soon the flowers will be dead and trees will be barren,
Then we will know that summer has fled.

And all nature around will seem asleep and forgotten;
Then the hearth by the fireside will welcome us home—
We can talk, we can ponder and think of the summer,
How we enjoyed the fragrance of its sweet-smelling bloom.

Alas! that is not all—the winter is coming
With its joy and its sorrow, its pleasure and pain,
And while wandering through winter with its snow storms and
    freezes
It seems but tomorrow that spring comes again.

Then spring-time appears, and is welcomed with gladness
By the bees and the birds and beasts of the field;
The flowers lift their heads to cheer man in his sadness,
And the birds sing sweet songs of the winter that has past.

Now our lives vary like the seasons in reason,
We are not all alike, and how could we be?
Some like the fall, always gloomy and chilly,
But once in awhile the sun shines in their home.

Now some like the winter—their lives are real stormy,
And it seems they are always looking for spring,
And they live in the hope of their spring-time coming;
And their winter will end like a dream on the wing.

Some like the spring, always glad and inviting,
And make all rejoice as they pass through this life,
And make one feel at home whene'er in their presence,
While waiting to welcome the summer to dawn.

Some like the summer, all gay like the flowers
That put out their blossoms in the sweet month of June,
And to meet them at home there is a glad hand of welcome
That makes one rejoice in their summer-like home.

OUR NOBLE BOOKER T. WASHINGTON

The greatest self-made man in the world today
Is one of our race, I am proud to say;
Not a giant in stature, nor robust in size,
But with brain and ambition he is noble and wise,
    Our noted Booker T. Washington.

By his great example and influence as well
He has brought the world to acknowledge him;
His noble ability, his manhood and pride,
With pluck and ambition also applied,
    Our noble Booker T. Washington.

Now today we applaud his great name with loud cheers,
In churches and halls and in Congress it appears
As well as in the schoolroom and our firesides so dear,
To the credit of our race we handle with care
    The name of Booker T. Washington.

We must always remember and should not forget
The poor little slave boy with just mother to pet,
He struggled through life with discouragements, yet
Determined abundance of knowledge to get,
    Our honorable Booker T. Washington.

Every mother in this country should teach her child
That with pluck and ambition, through hardships and trial,
And with strong determination and well made-up mind,
Through hard work and patience he can be in time
    The equal of Booker T. Washington.

MAN IS WHAT
HE WILLS TO BE

Man is what he wills to be—that is not a saying, but it is true;
I have had this experience, and it may be so with you,
Man need not worry about his fate, but let him take a stand;
It makes no difference what turns up, I will be a noble man.

And then he will work right to that end and every effort make
To build a towering monument to his credit grand and great,
And if he keeps on moving, doesn't stop to think of fate,
He will be the lucky man that the whole world calls great.

Then man is what he wills to be,
Either little, much or great;
He can make himself a world of power,
Or bring on a shameful fate.

I started out in life alone to win my way or die,
To make my life count something or would know the reason why,
And when the first effort had made discouraging and yet
I just put on a little pluck and pushed right to the gate.

Now it is more than a notion, fellowman, to take your place in
        life;
You have got to struggle hard and make a sacrifice,
But you feel better in the end when you look back and think
Of all the knocks you have undergone, and now your chain is
        linked.

Life is not worth living, fellow-woman, if you never have a lick,
You can appreciate success when it comes thick;
Sometimes I was up, sometimes I was down, and I would stop and
        think,
"This world is individuals, and each must take his place,"
I would brighten up and start afresh, and say "I will win the race."

So man is what he wills to be; God put him here to think,
Not like the dumb beast of the field, to only eat and drink,
He gave to man a glorious gift of knowing good from bad,
That he might be partaker of the good and scorner of the bad.

God gave man brain to think and faculties to act,
Gave him power to sail the seas and ride upon the winds,
To dive down in the mighty deep and bring up costly gems,
To dig the coal out of the earth that heats and gives us light,
And with a million other gifts I cannot name that is right.

MAY

One beautiful morning in the month of May all was serene and
     quiet,
The birds sang sweetly, their music a dream, and the sun shone
     bright;
The flowers all in bloom with their fragrance so sweet,
And the green-carpeted earth made the picture complete.

It was the first day of May, all nature seemed gay
And all of the trees seemed to bow and welcome the day,
And every heart seemed happy and the bees seemed to say,
"Do you know that winter has passed and this is the first day of
     May?"

When we think of San Francisco in her terror today,
We thank God we are living on the first day of May;
We have lots to be thankful for, and should continue to pray
For the sad ones in San Francisco on the first day of May.

PAY YOUR DEBTS

Everybody knows her, for they see her every day
As she swings around the corner with that blue dress on parade;

Though it is not all in looking, stylish clothes don't win today,
There's nothing counts like dollars when you have your debts to
     pay.

This we should teach our children, not extravagant to be,
As our race in this country has not so long been free;
They must take care of their money and buy homes in various
     ways,
To be creditable and honest when they have their debts to pay.

I believe in style and fashion that is not out of the way,
I believe in home and comfort and living happy every day;
Do not go beyond your means, makes no difference what they say,
And after awhile you will be excluded from having debts to pay.

Now this has been my motto, to do as well as say—
Not teach you and practice different, but I can truthfully say
That in my broad experience success has followed me,
And I make a strong effort to keep the debts all paid.

THE HOUSEHOLD OF RUTH

The Household of Ruth is pure friendship, love and truth,
It will keep you in your youth if you are a good attendant;
The law is strictly executed and lived up to by all
Who bear the name of the noble order,
And all is well with anyone who gets into her borders.

This organization is just what it should be,
Its principles for right and elevation
In carrying out the law in every form,
And this is what will make and save a nation.

It soothes the sister's broken heart with a loving word of cheer,
It fills the empty pocketbook of the needy one so drear,
It gives food to the hungry, takes care of the sick,
Buries its dead in order and all of those things, just think.

Why not join the Household above all other things?
When its principles are good and pure and its works so truly
    great,
Every man should be an Odd Fellow and every woman a Sister of
    Ruth;
They could not do better, now that is just the truth.

I AM AS HAPPY AS
A QUEEN ON HER THRONE

When I watch my two boys, Walter and Robert, at play,
It makes me think of my childhood days,
When I used to play and skip not alone as a mother,
    I am as happy as a queen on her throne.

With kind husband and children and comfortable home,
With Christ as our leader while through this world we roam,
Who never forsakes us or leaves us alone,
But shines as a light to beckon us on,
    I am as happy as a queen on her throne.

With pluck and ambition I have great success,
I make a strong effort and God does the rest,
I work for the future and think for the best,
And believe that my boys will make life a success,
    I am as happy as a queen on her throne.

Now when this life is ended on earth we love,
We hope to make a family in the kingdom above
Where all is joy, and peace, and love,
And then we will kneel and give God the praise,
    For he is our king on the throne.

WHAT IS WOMAN?

What is woman to the world? Has her worth been told?
It is true she is more precious than silver or gold,
Or rubies or diamonds; her worth cannot be told,
For she is a most precious jewel.

Then may it be ·emembered that she stands next to God,
If she lives for Christ's kingdom to take up her abode;
She was first at the cross and last at the tomb—
A faithful creature was woman.

And you will find her first in all good work,
And then when it is done you will find her always helping,
Too, to carry the burden of those she chances to meet,
Or her husband if she is a wife.

OCTOBER IS HERE

October is here, and the clubs begin business
After a sweet summer's rest from club work's toil and care;
Now afresh we begin preparing for winter,
To make happy hearts of the sad ones dear.

At last we thank God we are to do something to make
The world better by helping the poor; we ask God to guide us,
And give us ambition to bring food and comfort to many a door.

Yes, there are children awaiting our meeting that they may have
　　　clothes
And books for the school—they know where to get them;
The faithful club women are willing to give them help as a rule.

This is our club work, to give to the needy as well as improve
Our own minds, and to look after the sick and give homes
To the children, and tell the poor mother to tell hers what to do.

Now this is a great work we are doing, dear sisters,
Come, let us be united in doing what we can for the Lord,
Let us go hand in hand with each other, and remember as we lift
    let us climb.

In a few years we will be through with our meetings,
Then we will join the happy hosts o'er there with our Lord,
With our friends all around us and our Savior before us,
Standing to welcome us home in the end.

And then we will realize what good we have been doing
When life is no longer with us on this earth;
Let us take up new courage and hold fast to our promise,
We will receive our reward in the over-there.

As women of power and mothers of this country,
We must hold fast together to lift as we climb;
If we do not we will keep the race from uniting
And making one strong, united uplifting band.

GOD'S ELECTRIC POWER

The world with all of its thought and action
Is run by God's electric power;
We are God's improved invention,
He is promoter of the hour.

God is life and light and wisdom,
All that lives is built on him,
On the land and in the water,
The very air we breathe he gives.

Why should man be so egotistic
When he in God's sight is so like the clay;
But God has place for every creature
That in creation lives today.

He has seen fit to give us comfort,
And in peace and happiness to dwell,
If we obey his blest commandments
And do his everlasting will.

Why not make our lives impressive
By helping some one when we can,
And feel that we are each expected
To bring some credit to the land.

A RIOT

The Riot in Springfield, Ohio, February 26, 1906

When all was quiet and serene, a storm broke out at the dead,
And the roaring of pistols and firebells were heard;
On the sound of the midnight air could be heard
Loud voices screaming in agony great.

"Oh, what is the matter?" you could hear someone shout;
The answer, "My house is on fire! Someone put it out!"
Breathless the mob ran to and fro like a scout,
Putting torches and destruction to all that come about.

In the still of night, as horrible as death,
Comfortless and homeless so many were left
Hungry and clotheless in their awful flight;
Dear God, it was terrible at the dead hour of night!

This lawlessness has buried Springfield's great name,
But I hope business will go on just the same,
With her car-load of officers with salaries to pay
Not able to control this city today,
And we must be disgraced with a riot.

This is something awful in this great land today,
Where everything is prosperous and making a way,
To think peace is disturbed by the low and degraded,
And impeding progress by standing in the way
With their torches and pistols, taking the day with a riot.

O whiskey! that great evil that is doing it all,
But that is no excuse, let them answer the call
Of the strenuous law that is made for all,
And they will come to the conclusion when they have a fall
To be law-abiding citizens and courteous to all,
And there will be no more riot.

LIFE'S GOLDEN SUNSET

It's a grand thing when you're old, love,
   To have someone care for you,
Someone to make you happy,
   Someone to love you, too.

It makes life bright and gay, love,
   When you think of the summer flowers
That you used to nourish in childhood,
   In the spring of youth's hours

But oh, it's spring to me, love,
   When I look at your earnest gaze
And see the rosy sunbeams
   Upon your smiling face.

I would always be gay and happy, love,
   If I had you at my side,
It makes me revere the moment, love,
   When I became your happy bride.

But we are growing old, love,
   Our sun of life will soon set,

But as long as we are here, love,
　　We will bless the day we met.

So when toil and care are o'er, love,
　　And time with us will cease,
We will join that happy host, love,
　　Where all is joy and peace.

THE PROSPECT OF THE FUTURE,
Or
The Hand That Rocks the Cradle Rules the World

In looking o'er the prospects of the future
And knowing the success of the past,
And knowing it all comes through the woman of the world,
You need not count her least or last.

For all that you can count to your credit of being
This or that, or making life a success, you may rest assured
And it is true where're you go, that
The hand that rocks the cradle rules the world.

It seems that something must happen every day;
It takes a mother's tender care to drive the blues away,
It makes no difference how you try to keep her from the whirl,
She will let you know that the hand that rocks the cradle rules the
　　world.

We boast of our great president and statesmen grand and bold,
And forget it is through his mother's training
That his name has been enrolled among noble heroes;
Unfurling the flag and digging gold all come through
The hand that rocks the cradle rules the world.

COUNT YOUR BLESSINGS

If you would only stop to count your blessings
   I think we would more thankful be,
When we remember God is willing to give us
     blessings
   When we earn them full and free.

Do not let us stop to murmur
   When things go wrong and make you sigh;
Think this must come in a lifetime,
   Count your blessings, do not cry.

If we would only count our blessings
   How much happier we would be,
You know the loss is always counted,
But let them go for all they will bring
   In making happiness to thee.

CULTIVATION

We should cultivate our different tastes
And display them with modest grace;
Though all our tastes are not the same,
Of course we are not to blame.

But if we pursue the different arts
We will find a taste for something;
No matter what your taste may be,
Have courage to cultivate something.

We must find a taste for something—
Music, needlework or painting;
Each of these arts has its charm,
If you cultivate either 'twill do no harm.

Each one should strive hard
To find out what she can best do,
And when she finds her place
Fill it as if she always knew.

Everybody has a gift
If they did but know it,
And if you cultivate some taste
Your study will soon show it.

I studied the art of needlework,
And was soon adopted to it;
And as I studied farther on
I discovered that I was a poet.

I then and there began to write
And I am still sticking to it,
And some of the best critics in the land
Have indorsed me as a poet.

I believe in doing something good,
Why not? It is best to do it,
For you are adding to the world
If you only did but know it.

Now when we study Nature's law
It gives us thought and action,
Then we begin to realize
That we are God's invention.

TO THE QUEEN OF
THE BRITISH GOVERNMENT

To the queen of the British government
We owe gratitude and love
For giving our race liberty when coming in her gates;

She gave every man his portion and a home beneath her flag,
If he would be loyal and truthful, and stand up for the right.

Oh hail, the Queen of England! She was a royal queen indeed,
She was a queen to every nation, she was the nation's need;
She was an earthly angel, and full of love and pride;
For crushed, enslaved humanity she was a kind and loving guide.

Oh, that royal Queen of England! How we mourn her loss so
    great,
And to ever reverence her name, when we hear it spoke,
Of that God-given ruler, who made for us a place
That we might flee from evil to a home of refuge safe.

Her kingdom saved my father and gave him freedom sweet,
And I was born her subject, a Canadian complete;
But she has gone to the God that gave her, and we must give her
    up,
But her son, the King of England, has fallen heir to her throne,
With all of the royal honors King Edward now is crowned.

Now we hear the King of England is ill, and it grieves our hearts
    to know
That the son of the Queen of England's health is very poor;
Now, honored King of England, we love and adore your name,
For the sake of your dear old mother your kingdom I hope to
    hail.

Now we hope you will recover and live for years to come,
To make your kingdom happy as well as your royal home;
And I hope I may live to see you, as next year I expect to sail,
And with pride in that grand old country
And your kingdom I expect to hail.

Now, royal Queen Alexandria, I blush to speak your name,
To know my life's so humble and yours the heights of fame;
But as I am a woman and also a woman's friend, I read of you
And loved you as if I had met you time and again.

THE LAST DAY OF THE YEAR,
OR
NEW YEAR'S EVE

On the last day of the year we have so much to be thankful for,
So much we have had and so much that we should do,
To know that our lives have been spared here for something,
By One that knows the future, the present and past.

Let us prepare to meet the new year rejoicing,
To know that our lives have been spared for something good;
Let us make new resolutions to do more in the future
Than we have in the past for the kingdom of God.

Then each of our lives should be busy working
And thinking, and praying to God
To make the world better and men nobler and braver,
To take responsibilities and live up to his law.

We should be inspired to work for the Master,
In helping the sinner to come to his arms;
It is true this past year we have had struggles and crosses
As well as sunshine, and pleasure with pain.

But in life's weary dream this must all be expected,
But trusting will make the road easy to trod;
Then we are promised a great reward over yonder
With the glories and blessed in the kingdom of God.

When I think of our race in the past we have all things to hope
    for,
To know that God has prospered us so in the past;
We should be willing to trust him alone in the future,
And believe he will take us home when this life is past.

THE SILENT NIGHT

In the dead hour of night,
When all Nature is dreaming,
The watchman in the watch-tower
Is treading his beat.

The soft mellow breezes go out through the leaves,
The silvery moon peeps down through the trees;
It is the peaceful slumber of silent night,
When the earth is a most beautiful sight.

The countless stars in the heaven of light
Illumine the pilgrim's pathway bright
That speeds to and fro through the silent night,
In quest of a happier, holier plight.

Then he takes up new courage and travels right along,
The journey is long, but his faith is quite strong,
He knows that through hardships and struggle, if right,
He can cheerfully pass, with God, through the night.

It is like a dream of a cold winter night,
    When I think of the past;
The storm and cloud have left the skies
    And my pathway is clear at last.

GOSSIP

One fatal mistake that is made today is gossip;
Too many women, I am sorry to say, love to gossip.
The height of their ambition seems to be
To talk about their neighbor across the way
And to pick her to pieces as we commonly say, in gossip.

Find fault with her clothes, her husband or home,
Her style of living, her manner or brogue,

If not the poor girl who is struggling alone
To make for herself a comfortable home,
Or the boy that meets misfortune while through this world he
    roams,
Instead of simply gossip.

To gossip, my friend, is a terrible sin, it doesn't a fortune
For anyone win, but makes enemy and strife,
And wrecks some one's life and often breaks up homes,
And parts husbands and wives, and sometimes causes the use of a
    knife—
Then what is to blame but GOSSIP.

Now let us as club women do something else
To make the world better by looking at self
And talking of the things that make happiness and wealth,
And make ourselves useful for GOD and be blessed,
And be excused from GOSSIP.

OH WOMAN, BLESSED WOMAN!

Woman's worth to the world can never be told,
She is a jewel more needed than silver or gold,
The world could not move without her great name enrolled,
    Oh woman, blessed woman!

God created woman for the helpmate of man,
Knowing without woman man could not stand,
And then God devised a plan
To bring woman in existence from the rib of man,
    Oh woman, blessed woman!

Then God caused man to take a deep sleep,
And then his loving commandments to keep,
He would create something the pride of his life
And would make him happy by giving a wife,
    Oh woman, graceful woman!

You may find her busy in public and home,
In church work and club work she can plainly be seen,
In rearing her children each good mother a queen,
    Oh woman, blessed woman!

NEW YEAR'S MORNING, OR THE FIRST DAY OF THE YEAR

The new year has dawned and we meet it with gladness,
And today is a day of frolic and joy,
Notwithstanding some hearts are bowed down with sadness,
But we who are happy should pray for their joy.

I resolve today to make others happy and serve the great King
Who is supreme over all, to do all in my power
To make the world better by a Christian example
And answering when he calls.

This my forty-sixth New Year—I have been blest and lucky,
While others are gone and their voices hushed in death;
But I am here and spared to my family,
With my husband and children and friends to enjoy.

I look ahead away in the future, as well as thank God of love
For the past, to know when life is ended we have wound up
Our work here with hoping and trusting our Blessed Redeemer,
We'll bid farewell to earth and go home at last.

We should be careful in rearing our children and teach them the
    things
That will add to their lives, that will inspire them to think,
And act for the Master, and share responsibilities of this life's
    great burden,
And feel it is a duty they must perform.

I could say more, though it gives me pleasure to know
I have lived through sadness and sorrow as well as pleasure and
    pain;

I know what it is to be sad and heart-broken, but trusting God
Has brought peace and happiness again.

LET US STRIVE TO DO SOMETHING

Let us strive to do something inspiring,
Let us strive to do something for God,
Let us strive to make somebody happy,
For this is our duty to all.

Now this is the work of a Christian,
To lift up the weak ones that fall,
To help them to carry their burden
To the Lamb that gives comfort to all.

Let us take heed and be anchored
In this Rock that cannot shake or will not fall;
The Savior that is always our refuge
Let us answer at once when he calls.

He will be our food when we are hungry,
He will be our drink when we are dry,
He will be our peace in confusion,
He will take us home by and by.

Let us be true to each other,
For this is our Savior's command,
Strive hard to do our whole duty
And receive our reward in the end.

OUR CLUB WORK

To better the condition of humanity,
For the cultivation of the mind,
To tear down the walls of ignorance,
Then we are lifting as we climb.

To make sacrifice a pleasure,
　We will see results in time;
If we only work and trust God
　He will reward us after while.

So let us make work pleasure,
　And never murmur, never fear,
But take Christ for our leader,
　And always keep him near.

Now as long as he will lead us
　Not a battle will we lose in line;
Then we will work and trust him ever
　In this lifting as we climb.

Now, dear sisters, when we are weary
　And all burdened down with care,
With the club work we have been doing
　In lifting others here,

We will bind our sheaves together,
　As club women true and tried,
Then we will look alone to Jesus,
　Who will give us our reward.

AN ORPHAN GIRL

I am a little orphan girl,
　My ma and pa are dead;
The Phyllis Wheatley mamas me
　And gives me what I need.

They give me pretty clothes to wear,
　And books to read I love;
May long life and success bless
　The Phyllis Wheatley Culture Club.

All little girls are not like me blessed,
To have someone to care for them
When their parents are at rest,
But the Phyllis Wheatley has seen fit to take me in their breast.

THE CHURCH BELLS

List, I hear the church bells ring,
They sound like distant music to me,
I love to go to church and hear the choir sing
The beautiful praises of God.

My heart is glad when the Sabbath appears,
Then I make preparations for church,
I sometimes wish Sabbath would last all the year,
For it drives away sorrow and grief.

My life has been cloudy, with sunshine and rain,
But I will just take that for my lot, and feel that
I am no better than Jesus my king,
And they crucified him on the cross.

SCRAPS OF TIME

Time has brought about great changes,
    And will bring as many more;
Now to waste time it is dangerous,
    For time is precious, but always sure.

Now time is so very precious,
    Just one moment at a time,
Then we should always improve it
    As it gently passes by.

Now we will take time for pleasure,
  And we must take time for pain;
And let us spend our spare moments' time
  In brightening up the mind.

Let us get good books and read them,
  So that we may be inspired
To put our time in something good,
  To show what we have read.

Now time belongs to God the father,
  And he deals it out to man,
Just as he sees fit to give it;
  But with God time never ends.

But with man time has a limit,
  And sometime it is very short,
But the main thing is to improve it;
  While you have time do your part.

You can do that in thought or action,
  Or in work in various ways;
The slave has proven this to you
  By accomplishing something in his day.

He was styled alone as chattels,
  In this country now so great,
But time has made him famous,
  For he put Christ in the lead.

Then Christ fought for him his battle,
  And broke the chain that set him free,
And time has made him the greatest man
  The whole world knows today.

Just in forty years of freedom
  He has made this country think;
He is styled inventor, doctor, lawyer,
  And proficient in every rank.

And this is not half—contractor,
　　Soldier brave, and in battle he stands first;
And he's owner of great properties,
　　And has millions in his purse.

This country should be proud of him
　　And make him a welcome guest.
It might as well, for he is here to stay,
　　And is still feathering his nest.

THE WAYWARD SON

Good-by, my son, good-by,
My poor wayward boy!
You are breaking your poor father's heart;
He loves you, and believed
That you would mend your way
And would from bad habits depart.

But alas, it seems hopeless, hopeless,
When I think of you now a man,
And still seem perfectly contented
With throwing your earnings to the winds.

Stop and think for a moment!
Your time is fair spent, and soon life
With you will be at a close;
You had better be saving your earnings
For something that will do you good.

You will soon be counted with men and things of the past,
And nothing to your credit will note when you are spoken of by
　　name;
The world will only laugh, for they won't even remember your
　　name.

Now you cannot be a back number with your intellect and brain;
Save your time and credit and put your earnings out to work,
And say, "I will have something and show the world I am a man."

Then you will make your father happy
When he thinks, "My son has accomplished
To make my old age brighter,
And give me happiness in the end.

"I have worked and toiled and struggled
To give him all of the chance to stand
Side by side with any hero in this broad and noted land;
He can get to be a hero and make himself a noble man,"

Now if you will stop and think,
My son, what God expects of you,
You will surely turn around
And find something good to do

That will make your name a credit
And will drown the awful past,
And make me feel so proud of you
To know that you are a creditable man at last.

THE PARTING LOVERS

Good-by, sweetheart, our days of bliss,
Sealed by love's pure and sacred kiss,
Are ended in tears;
We part—the dream is o'er,
    Good-by, sweetheart.

I may not meet thee of old,
But oh, how can we live apart,
God knoweth best, God help us both
To live and say
    Good-by, sweetheart.

DO YOUR BEST

When you are called on to perform a duty,
  Do your best;
Make an effort to fill the pace,
  And God will do the rest.
Never say, "That is too hard for me,"
But always try to make the task
A world of pleasure.
  Do you know why?
Because God has put you here
For something good and grand;
If you cannot fill the pace
Will you have answered the command?

MARRIAGE VOW

May God bless your home
And make you happy;
May he children to you give,
May your union prove a blessing,
Teaching others how to live.

Always keep your marriage sacred,
Then you never will grow cold,
But will always love each other
Until death will part you all.

God invented happy union,
God indorses marriage vows;
Then let no one put asunder
What God has given to you now.

THE SUN OF OUR EXISTENCE

The sun of our existence here
   Is sinking very fast,
Let us make our lives a monument
   Of credit while we last.

Let us do all of the good we can,
   That others may see and feel
That we made the word better
   By ambition, pluck and zeal.

Let it be our hearts' desire to make history
   While we live, so that others may retain
And know that we have accomplished something
   And also lived to live again.

Each of us should be inventors
   In this broad and busy land,
And feel it is our duty
   To be improving all of the time.

Let us give the world new ideas,
   And exercise our hands and brain,
As coming generations will expect of us
   To learn something grand and something
Noble of our action in this age.

Now as we must fill our places
   Let us fill them with delight and feel this is our gain,
You know success follows labor just as pleasure follows pain.

Let us then be up and doing
   What we find, with all of our might,
In this business world improving
   And leaving monuments of light.

THE WOULD-BE CRITIC

Very often when you are striving
To make life a grand success,
Someone stands off and criticises
By giving you the discouraging laugh.

But what need you care for that!
Just keep the upward road,
And this will lead you to success,
If you ambitiously onward go.

The one that laughs the loudest
Is the one that laughs the last,
So when you see them laughing
Just put on more ambition to the task.

And tell them you are a hero,
And expect to win the prize;
That you mean to be a champion
In whatever you undertake.

No prize comes very easy,
You must work and fight to win;
That is why the Japs are fighting hard
And the Russians losing them.

God is not always with the strongest,
But is always with the right.
That is why the Japanese won;
He gave them power and might.

Now this should be a lesson
For this country great and grand,
That God is no respecter of persons,
But is father of every man.

It is a very dangerous thing
To undertake to crush the weak;
For our Savior is always on their side—
As a general thing they are meek.

THE BIRD SONG

The little birds warble their song in the tree,
Chee-chee, whee-whee, whee-whee;
Their song is the sweetest music to me,
Chee-chee, whee-whee, whee-whee.

In the morning you hear them sing before day,
Especially in the beautiful mornings of May,
When flowers are all blooming with fragrance so sweet,
And the earth represents a glorious green sheet.

Then our hearts all rejoice that winter has flown,
And spring has appeared in it's beautiful gown,
To make the heart happy of the sad and forlorn,
Then you will hear the birds singing their song.

When we think of the birds and the loving care
That God gives them through the winter and spares them to sing,
And much more attention he has given to man.

Why not love God and trust him as only man can,
And he will teach us to sing in that beautiful land
Sweeter songs than the birds ever sang.

Now evening appears and the birds' songs are hushed,
They have flown to the trees and couched in their nests,
They have spent a remarkable day.

Just as the birds' little voices are hushed,
Just so will ours in the night of our lives,

And may it be said of us just as of the birds,
That we have made someone happy today.

This world is a forest, a flower field, a grove,
And it is tenderly cared for by love,
God is the father of this beautiful land,
And dwells with the angels above.

Let us make it our business to be like the birds,
To make every heart happy we meet,
Then when time is no longer with us on the earth
We will worship at our Savior's feet.

THE MISSIONARY

I think at a distance I hear a loud voice,
Saying, Come, Come, Come.
Look unto me and I will make you rejoice,
Come, Come, Come.

It is the cry of the father to the heathen so great,
He waits us as missionaries to bring them to his feet,
Then he says Come, Come, Come.

Now why will you linger, or why will you wait,
If you are cleansed they cannot hurt you, then bring them
    to me,
I say Come, Come, Come.

The world will grow better, if you do your part
In helping the sinner whenever you can,
You can do it if you will, that is Christ's command,
Then Come, Come, Come.

TELL HER SO

If you have a word of cheer,
That will light the pathway drear
Of a pilgrim sister here,
 Tell her so.
Tell her you appreciate
What she does and do not wait
Till the heavy hand of fate
 Lays her low.
If your heart contains a thought,
That will brighter make her lot,
Then in mercy, hide it not—
 Tell her so.
Wait not till your friend is dead,
Ere your compliments are said,
For the spirit that has fled,
 (If it knows)
Does not need, where it has gone,
That poor praise to speed it on;
There love's endless, golden dawn,
 Is a glow.
But unto our sister here
That poor praise is very dear;
If you have a word of cheer,
 Tell her so.

LONELY WORLD

Sometime the world seems sad and lonely
 To the weary passer-by,
For he has a heavy burden,
 That is the reason why.

Something sad to him has happened
  On his journey home,
But this to him may prove a blessing
  As he goes further on.

The negro in this country thought
  That his lot was very hard,
To know his lot was cast in bondage
  But he put his full trust in the Lord,

And like all other work he does
  He heard the mournful prayers;
He heeded them, he answered them,
  And in his time he set the captive free.

ALL WE ASK IS JUSTICE

The Ohio Federation is a grand and glorious band
Of noble colored women who invade this fatherland;
They have taken a grand stand in making a demand
For their offspring of this land justice.

They are making a great sacrifice, but mean to win the prize;
Makes no difference what it costs them they mean to live or try
To make the future better, or they will know the reason why;
The only thing they're asking now is justice.

We will let the awful past alone and act as we call wise;
We are willing to work hard and make most any sacrifice
Or do anything we can to help our race to rise,
But all we ask at any hands is justice.

We feel that we are right in making this demand,
Our fathers worked and shed their blood to make this country
    grand;
They have fought in every battle and are willing yet to stand,
And all they ask this country now is justice.

We think at last we have a friend in Roosevelt, the president;
He stands for right, a hero bold, as he knows all races have a
    soul,
As chief executive of this land he makes this stern and last
    demand,
And means it, too—for every man justice.

As women of Ohio state we open up a broader gate,
And ask each state to federate, and this will make us stronger;
When every state is organized and all are fighting for this prize;
Then you will hear our women loudly cry, we must have justice.

PAUL LAURENCE DUNBAR

One of our race's great lights has gone out to the world,
No more he will flourish his pen with a whirl,
As a poet he'll live and shine like a star,
In the hearts of his race, Paul Laurence Dunbar.

Yes, he has answered the call that comes to us all,
Only young, it is true, but his life's work is done,
Though his name will live and shine like the sun,
As though his life had just begun. Our noted, Paul Laurence
    Dunbar.

Is he missed, yes he's missed in the hearts of his friends.
    And that mother that loved and watched o'er him to the end,
Is sad and heart-broken that you may depend,
When she thinks of Paul Laurence Dunbar.

Our Savior that cares for the beast and the birds,
Will tenderly care for that mother on earth,
That has brought such a treasure to the credit of her race,
As our noble, Paul Laurence Dunbar.

Now when he is laid in his last resting place,
And followed with sad hearts, bathed in tears,

It will long be remembered, years upon years,
The death of Paul Laurence Dunbar.

Springfield, Ohio, February 14, 1906.

GOLDEN JUBILEE OF WILBERFORCE

Oh! Wilberforce, our star of hope,
    We love and adore thy name;
Many find knowledge within thy courts
    And are wielding a sword of fame.

Just think in a half century,
    How proud we ought to be,
Of a noted place like Wilberforce,
    Sound aloud the jubilee.

Long live the name of Wilberforce,
    May she shine as bright as the sun,
At the end of a whole century,
    As if she had just begun.

Many bring credit to this our race,
    From thy broad and open doors,
They hail from South America
    And from Africa's dark shores.

They come from foreign countries,
    They come from the isles of set,
To be taught at our noted Wilberforce
    And to the olden Jubilee.

Let us strive to do something for Wilberforce,
    And add to her great name more;
With her towering halls and libraries,
    And her museum a perfect store.

With her choir of heavenly voices,
    Giving God's great name all praise,
With ambition, brain and honor
    Her students take this day.

With culture and refinement,
    With modesty and grace,
With push, pluck and ambition,
    Each student fills his place.

Three cheers for our dear old Wilberforce,
    Three cheers for its faculty brave,
Three cheers for its loyal president,
    Three cheers for its heroes in the grave.

Can we forget the founder,
    Of this grand and noted place?
Dear Bishop Payne the hero,
    May his ashes rest in peace.

Not only him but others,
    That have gone to their resting place,
And their soul with God that giveth,
    All happiness and peace.

TO THE CONFERENCE

Another conference year has passed,
    And we are yet alive;
Our lots not with the dead are cast,
    For Heaven we all strive.

Dear bishops, what a privilege
    To deal with God in prayer,
To send His shepherds to the field
    For loving flocks to care.

May God inspire your heart to work
   In vineyards day and night,
And with Him only for you shield
   To take up arms and fight.

May you take new courage now
   To conquer in the fight,
With God as refuge in your front,
   Make Satan take his flight.

And when you in new fields have gone
   And the gospel you have proclaimed,
And bade poor sinners come to Christ,
   To\love and praise His name.

When you have finished your work on earth,
   And the Master has called you home,
May your life be spent in saving souls,
   Then you will have overcome.

May we all meet on yonder shore,
   Where conference never ends,
With Christ as bishop at the head,
   And we His children blest.

Dear bishops, then your work will cease;
   Dear ministers, then you'll rest,
And all of whom have kept the faith
   Will go home and be blest.

THIS COUNTRY'S NEEDS

This country needs more noble men
   That will stand for God and right;
That, willingly, their aid will lend,
   To stop this country's fight.

More sun crowned men, that fear the Lord,
   That will the law, enforce.
More men, that read and love his word—
   Men, that pursues this course.

More men of principle and prayer,
   Not men that wants a name.
More men working for the cause
   And not for worldly fame.

But men that are willing to sacrifice,
   To help this country's needs.
Men that will stand up alone—
   Their loving lord, to please.

We want more men that studies law
   That will the law, obey,
That will shudder at the thought of crime
   In any form or way.

Men not afraid to trust the Lord.
   That will take Him at His Word—
That will own Him in their offices
   And His name in their homes be heard.

And in election time not beer and wine
   Should control the voting polls.
Let principle with good and right—
   Not, friends, silver nor gold.

Then peace will reign all over the land
   And men will do the right.
Then take God for your guide and shield
   and He will stop the fight.